THE COMMERCIAL EXPLOITATION OF ABUSE

THE COMMERCIAL EXPLOITATION OF ABUSE

A Study on Policy

Peter Fritz Walter

Published by Sirius-C Media Galaxy LLC

Business Filings Incorporated

108 West 13th St., Wilmington, DE 19801, USA

Essays on Law, Policy and Psychiatry, Vol. 8

Set in Avenir Light and Trajan Pro

Designed by Peter Fritz Walter

ISBN 978-1-984066-70-1

Publishing Categories
Psychology / Social Psychology

Publisher Contact Information
publisher@sirius-c-publishing.com
http://sirius-c-publishing.com

Author Contact Information
pfw@peterfritzwalter.com

About Dr. Peter Fritz Walter
http://peterfritzwalter.com

Parallel to an international law career in Germany, Switzerland and the United States, Dr. Peter Fritz Walter (Pierre) focused upon fine art, cookery, astrology, musical performance, social sciences and humanities.

He started writing essays as an adolescent and received a high school award for creative writing and editorial work for the school magazine.

After finalizing his law diplomas, he graduated with an LL.M. in European Integration at Saarland University, Germany, in 1982, and with a Doctor of Law title from University of Geneva, Switzerland, in 1987.

He then took courses in psychology at the University of Geneva and interviewed a number of psychotherapists in Lausanne and Geneva, Switzerland. His interest was intensified through a hypnotherapy with an Ericksonian American hypnotherapist in Lausanne. This led him to the recovery and healing of his inner child.

After a second career as a corporate trainer and personal coach, Pierre retired in 2004 as a full-time writer, philosopher and consultant.

His nonfiction books emphasize a systemic, holistic, cross-cultural and interdisciplinary perspective, while his fiction works and short stories focus upon education, philosophy, perennial wisdom, and the poetic formulation of an integrative worldview.

Pierre is a German-French bilingual native speaker and writes English as his 4th language after German, Latin and French. He also reads source literature for his research works in Spanish, Italian, Portuguese, and Dutch. In addition, Pierre has notions of Thai, Khmer, Chinese, Japanese, and Vietnamese.

All of Pierre's books are hand-crafted and self-published, designed by the author. Pierre publishes via his Delaware company, Sirius-C Media Galaxy LLC, and under the imprints of IPUBLICA and SCM (Sirius-C Media).

The author's profits from this book are being donated to charity.

CONTENTS

Introduction

What was first, love or abuse? It seems to me that love was first, as love is the natural condition.

In a society that has forgotten about love, however, it is not astonishing to see scientists and researchers, instead of being concerned with the question of *love*, being assiduously focused on *abuse* instead. It's very similar with Western medicine that equally is focused only upon the pathological, instead of finding out what *health* is actually about.

Where love itself has become the anathema of the day, how can we wonder that those who engage in it are associated with the devil? Where life has lost its wholeness, where love is schizophrenically split into acceptable behavior and unacceptable behavior, people tend to create fictitious concepts in a virtual reality of fake-values.

It seems that only poets and lovers are able to see through the thick layers of hypocrite life denial that is currently the invisible paradigm of the majority of humanity—at least in the part of the world that has incorporated postmodern international consumer culture as its new credo and lifestyle.

Where erotic love is equated with abduction and abuse, there is only one step to end up in hysteria—individually and collectively. Western society has done that step, and thoroughly! It has ended up not only in hysteria, but in *public paranoia*. Today we should do a retrospection and ask how this was at all possible, after Freud?

And how it's possible that after the turn into the millennium we ended up in the Middle-Ages?

Timewave Zero, it is true, shows us cyclic patterns in human evolution—and it indeed shows that the present times are most closely related to the early Middle-Ages. But the time-lined view of human history hides the spiraled growth patterns that go along with all evolution.

—See, for example, the interesting study of Hanspeter Seiler entitled 'Spiralform, Lebensenergie und Matriarchat', in: Nach Reich: Neue Forschungen zur Orgonomie,

INTRODUCTION

Frankfurt/M: 2001 Verlag, 1997, pp. 411-443. Following an initial research idea by Wilhelm Reich on the spiral and the spiraled form of all human evolution, the author shows in this article that early Mediterranean cultures were abounding in their symbolism of the spiral, and that even conservative archeologists in the meantime acknowledge that the spiral is a symbol for fertility and growth. The author shows that the cosmic life energy forms spontaneously spiraled patterns, which can be seen in many natural manifestations and forms, such as galaxies, snail house and mussel shell patterning, enzymes, electromagnetic currents, amoeboid structures, until the form of our DNA.

When we progress, this is not a linear movement, but a spiraled one because the spiral is the only form in nature that ideally combines the line with the circle.

And when we advance, we not only relocate farther but also higher. While the line leaves its root, the circle stays with it, and the spiral, while advancing, carries its root along. When that happens, we are again within that pattern, but at a higher level of it. This means that we have more chances now, and are instrumental for dealing with the pattern effectively, and perhaps dissolve it completely.

What kind of pattern is that?

Astrologically it is the *Pisces* archetype, as opposed to the *Aquarius* archetype. It is a pattern of energies that puts the collective, the group and the majority's rules, opinions and feelings higher than the individual's. It values the group before it values the individuals who compose the group. It considers standard solutions before it considers intelligent solutions. It fears the marginal and the original and blesses uniformity and herd thinking. Its educational paradigm is one of mass indoctrination and mass alphabetization. It educates by disempowering the child, and by using threat and authority-based hierarchy, and strong competition. It basically positions the human being as opposed to nature or as *master over nature* and, as a result, is rather hostile toward the child's expressing their natural emotions, feelings and desires.

This paradigm is the reigning educational paradigm of the great monotheistic religions and it often serves for justifying ritual abuse and even the torture of children as a disciplinary measure and in the name of some religious authority, savior or leader. Now, what we face, especially in controversial matters of public discussion is a resistance that operates in the masses' collective consciousness because of their fear to progress into the unknown. This unknown is not so unknown after all. It's the *Aquarius* paradigm.

The *Aquarius Age* will definitely be one of more individuality and more democracy, and more choice at every level of life. The Aquarian energy which is the energy of the planet Uranus, as opposed to the Neptunian energy that reigns Pisces, will help us face and confront rather then repress our hitherto unconscious desires and render them conscious so that we can deal with them on a more rational basis.

We will then be able to see love as love and abuse as abuse, or love as encompassing erotic love *(erós)* and abuse as a form of psychological, physical or sexual distortion that is created by *repression* and acted out in a violent manner.

To see this will render us sensitive to the fact that non-violent and consenting forms of love are not abuse. Only a society that is highly confused about its own value system can come up with the kind of arbitrary assumptions that today pervade the entire public discussion about abuse, especially in the puritanical Anglo-Saxon world with its long tradition of life denial, sexual repression, body-and-touch anxiety and physical, sexual, domestic and structural violence. As long as one is part of the wheel, turning with the crazy machinery of a paranoid society, one cannot really grasp the psychological implications of what Krishnamurti called *Freedom from the Known.*

It is impossible to perceive truth when one has been brainwashed for years or even decades, obediently consuming the lukewarm soup of standard media gossip with its half-truths, its hypocrisies and its false securities. It is absolutely impossible if one is not motivated by some kind of inner Kantian imperative that says a definite *No* to all this at a certain point of time, followed by a clear decision to remain, at least for a few years, if not for life, *untelevisioned, unchurched and unnewspapered.*

It took me about thirty years to get away from ingesting this dangerous soup and to begin perceiving what it means to be myself! If I had not taken this essential diet, I could not even dream of writing this guide, let alone publish it and stand for it in a highly aggressive, non-comprehensive, manipulative and violent society that has lost its humanity long ago. What credit can we grant a society that goes out to kill, in drug wars, wars for so-called democracy and witch hunts of various kinds, that maintains intelligence services that engage in abuses worse than all it projects onto its scapegoat groups, and that lets more than half of its scientists work for the military? What can we expect from a society that calls itself enlightened and that has enacted the most revolutionary Constitution of the world, that publicly unveils fascist and terrorist regimes, yet practices, under this very Constitution, exactly, and worse, what those regimes do?

> —In international law, the Constitution of the United States of America, adopted in its original form on September 17, 1787 by the Constitutional Convention in Philadelphia, is generally acclaimed to represent the first and foremost example of a freedom-loving and citizen-empowering enactment of a modern democratic nation that can serve as a sample for other nations. In fact, after being defeated in World War II, Germany has received, from the side of the allies and their Constitutional Commission, a Grundgesetz or Verfassung (Verfassung means Constitution in German language) that was tightly drafted after the Constitution of the United States of America, and that is often cited as the second example of a modern constitution that is based on the fundamental guarantees of human rights, due process and civil liberties.

Should it not be a good moment to wake up from the thousand-and-first nightmare of public and pretendedly scientific cover-up and turn to your inner voice that knows the truth, if only you got enough civil disobedience to listen to it? I believe it is so difficult for most of us because of our past that favors male supremacy, monotheism and what Joseph Campbell called the *Murder of the Goddess.*

To secure the paradigm of parental control that is the exact pendant to an all-pervasive punitive and jealous male Gee-Oh-Dee, a set of values is inflicted upon the community that publicly and legally denies children's rights and power to decide for their own bodies and their own pleasures as far as love is concerned—*while icecream is allowed.* Icecream and plastic toys, industrially produced for the child that is not allowed to accept their body as a pleasure organ—that it of course originally is—are among the most powerful conditioning devices of modern society. They ensure that the human being is transformed into a consumerist robot that is needed for the functioning of a robot society.

An abuse-centered culture needs abuse to happen. It will unconsciously turn events in such a way that what it silently and openly predicts will eventually happen. I am convinced that much abuse came about as the result of self-fulfilling prophecies and a generally very negative outlook upon life—and the lack of creativity that results from such a stiffening point of departure.

Instead, people tend to invoke the *good old times* which represents the most stupid argument ever brought forth in human history. This kind of statements are psychological chewing-gum. They keep people fixated upon the past, rendering them unable to live in the present and thus unable to solve present problems. It is the strategy of the fascist worldview that always operates on an irrational level while manipulating the masses into accepting fake-solutions that sound grandiose but in reality represent old errors in a new costume, or no solutions at all.

Thus, after this short look over the fence, you may quickly see that society, or the main and obvious part of it, will not help you to heal your own distorted emotional setup, and will not be of help for you to become, for example, a good enough parent.

—Bruno Bettelheim (1903-1990) was an Austrian-born American writer and child psychologist. He is widely known for his studies of autism. The most significant part of Bettelheim's professional life was spent serving as director of the Sonia Shankman Orthogenic School at the University of Chicago, a home for emotionally disturbed children. He wrote books on child psychology and was respected by many during his lifetime. His book The Uses of Enchantment recast fairy tales in terms of Freudian psychology. It was awarded the U.S. Critic's Choice Prize for criticism in 1976 &

the National Book Award in the category of Contemporary Thought in 1977. See Bruno Bettelheim, A Good Enough Parent, New York: Vintage Books, 1988, and The Uses Of Enchantment, New York: Vintage Books, 1989.

And if this society, that seems to hide much more than it reveals and admits to be true, is so outright judgmental that it tears down even those who have the best intentions, but touch the taboo, then you will stop looking for solutions here. Then perhaps you will turn inside and look of you can become *resourceful* by yourself and develop a set of tools that will help you achieve your goal of healing yourself. Or you may turn to somebody who has done it before you, such as myself.

In the next sub-chapter, I will have a look at an interesting word, a word that I consider to be *symptomatic* for all the content that this present society, because of lacking understanding, projects on certain individuals in order to demonize them, which in turn transforms these poor individuals into *lighting catchers* for the abysmal discharges of pent-up and misdirected energies that the collective ignorance produces for the whole of society.

CHAPTER ONE

Child Protection

When we talk about *child protection*, we talk about a modern paradigm, a concept that was mainly developed in the 20th century, while the idea was present already in early Christianity. As Susanne Cho demonstrated in her doctoral thesis, the idea of child protection seems to be unthinkable before about the second half of the 17th century.

—Susanne Cho, Kindheit und Sexualität im Wandel der Kulturgeschichte: Eine Studie zur Bedeutung der kindlichen Sexualität unter besonderer Berücksichtigung des 17. und 20. Jahrhunderts, Zürich, 1983 (Doctoral thesis).

This is so because it was at that moment in human history that, for the first time, it was defined what a *child* is—while before that period children were not considered as a separate race that obeys to different laws. It does not surprise in fact that it was exactly with the starting point of consumerist thinking that the idea came up that children had to be regulated and held tight. The underlying promise was that children represented tremendously important consumers. Hence, the idea of protection, which finds its parallel in slave holding, which was on the rise from exactly the same point in history. Slaves, too, had to be protected—mainly from running away.

Considering this fundamental shift in perspective regarding the importance of the child for the welfare of the economy is essential for understanding our present child protection paradigm. In fact, all our age of consent laws are based on the fictional definition of *the child.* Without a person being considered *a child,* age of consent laws do not apply.

Child is thus a legal criterion. This is of tremendous importance for the understanding of the why and how of our *child protection* laws. So I need to dig a little deeper and find out what a *child* is under the definition of the law. And when I look through existing age of consent laws I may be surprised to find one single criterion: the *age* of the child. No mention of maturity, no mention of knowledge about life or former experience, no mention of IQ, no mention of the will of the child. All this is considered irrelevant by modern child protection laws. A child is a person below the age of consent. The age of consent is so and so many years. And how many years it is, actually depends on time and place, and on the cultural setting. Thus, we can conclude at this point that the ultimate purpose of our age of consent laws is to protect a certain age-group of people from experiencing sex or body pleasure.

The rationale of age of consent laws, and ultimately of child protection, may not be clear. It has to be elucidated. The answers we get from our law makers and from our child-protection experts are clear-cut. Sex is something for adults, we hear. Sex is damaging the child, we hear. Children are *sexually innocent*, we hear, and have to be protected from abuse. This is the official rhetoric.

I wonder if we are not all innocent about driving cars until we get our driver's license? I once dated a student girl who was sexually *innocent* at age twenty-one. Does that mean that at age twenty-one, she was still a child? According to the laws of consent, she was an adult. Yet she was a virgin and said she had suffered from the fact that all through her childhood her mother had forbidden her to touch herself, that her mother had regularly followed her up to the toilet to make sure that she was 'not touching herself.' This student girl was an incarnation of guilt and shame, and she said she felt attracted only to old men, to men who physically looked like her father. Upon my inquiry why she did not find men of her age attractive, she replied that she found young men *brutal and insensitive.* This young woman may be an exception or she may have suffered from a particularly harsh and life-denying education, but cases like hers let us question the rationale of *morality.* It is often argued in conservative circles of society that children should by no means be sexually awakened as this would impair their sense of morality. Now, then, let us inquire into this argument. First of all, which morality is meant? Is it the morality of good behavior, of decency, of moral conduct, of respecting others? Does that mean so far that the child has to abstain from sex so as to learn to respect other people, so as to keep a good conduct and learn a decent behavior? Indeed, it is argued in conservative circles that children had to pass a certain time for learning, and not just for enjoying life, and that too much of body pleasure and enjoyment was detrimental to their sense of morality; that children had to encounter some hardship and learn to deprive themselves of certain things that they could enjoy *later on* in life.

Does that mean the child must abstain from sex for the common good, for the sake of morality? Or for their own good? If the first is true, we are not talking about child protection, but about morality protection, or the protection of that strange thing that in legal textbooks is referred to as *public morals*. If the second is true, we are dealing with a paradigm of child protection that applies restrictions to the child's life for the best of the child.

The present study will try to elucidate what the current state of the law is in matters of child protection and how age of consent laws have grown historically, what their rationale is, and how, or not, they serve the child's welfare. I will also comment on some of the rather folkloristic and irrational aspects of the present public child abuse debate and the character structure of people who stress child protection with particular emphasis, exhibiting an almost obsessed focus on the protective stance in education. This is to say that in such an intensely controversial debate, to abstain from any judgment and pretending to deliver an 'objective' assessment of the topics at stake would be an illusory and perhaps dishonest endeavor. I want to see the person who can react cold-bloodedly to such a hot matter. Children's fate does trigger deep emotions, and for good reason.

Yet, not only because I am a lawyer and therefore perhaps more detached when looking at things that shock most people, I would like to invite the reader to try hard to steer in between the extreme positions of the child protectors, on one hand, and the self-declared *pedophiles*, on the other. Because probably on neither of these sides, truth may reside, because the positions are extreme by themselves. And they have probably become even more extreme over the last few years because of an evident lack of dialogue, let alone good-willed and constructive interaction, between these groups of people.

This is why I would like to expose in this book some of the absurdities that are to be found in the rhetoric of both the child protectors and the declared and organized pedophiles on the matter of loving children. And what about listening to the children themselves? I have done so and this inquiry led to some fundamental insights that are not brought forth by both the child protectors and the organized pedophiles. In addition I would like to come up with some perhaps original ideas about how children could be protected in a way that leaves their emotional integrity as untouched as possible. I am going to call this idea *principle of non-intervention* and it's not a new idea, but a recurrent argument in the writings of alternative child psychologists such as the late French child therapist Françoise Dolto or the American child psychologist Alayne Yates. Else, some women rights activists such as Stevi Jackson have taken a strong stance on freeing the child's sex life from an overhead of paternalistic control and regulation.

—See, for example, Françoise Dolto, La Cause des Enfants (1985), Stevi Jackson, Childhood and Sexuality (1986) and Alayne Yates, Sex Without Shame: Encouraging the Child's Healthy Sexual Development (1978).

I admit that, while this study was first elaborated as a purely legal analysis, it grew and expanded over time because I did not want to blind out my own emotional reaction to the whole of this subject. I did this because I believe that our emotions are intelligent, and often even more than our minds. And thus I concede that my position is partly subjective and does not pretend to be a dry professional analysis. By the way, in the rather large bibliography, you will find a number of such rather statistical assessments and case reports, if you are interested in that. I just could not silence my heart, looking at these matters only with my intellectual mind, and as a result my heart sometimes speaks louder than my intellect.

The reader may forgive me this bias, but without allowing myself to express my sometimes a bit extreme contradiction of the current standard opinions on the matter, this study would never have been published.

As my first multi-disciplinary research on the matter started back in 1985, it has been twenty-one years flowing in the land before I considered this manuscript mature enough to be born as a published book.

CHAPTER TWO

Sex Offender

The expression *sex offender* associates a kind of sexual heresy. Offending—what or whom? When I have offended a person sexually I am still not a sex offender and remain a person offender. I cannot offend *sexuality*, can I? Can you offend the sun?

The expression targets at persons who actually offend the reigning paradigm of sexuality which is exactly the Church's traditional view of heresy. The Church, in its hybrid arrogance to define what was life and what was not, said there was good sex and bad sex. It more precisely said that all sex was bad but granted a tight exception for procreation. So as to say it judged Gee-Oh-Dee severely, saying that *He was an idiot* to have created man with various sensual desires that it could just not fit under its provincial fascist mindset. In saying that, at the root of its life paradigm, sex was bad, the Church said basically that life was bad. Sex is life, isn't it? How can life come about without sex?

To regulate man's pleasures was a powerful and tyrannical means to subdue the population under the Church's exclusive power. Nothing is more effective for manipulating and dominating man than prohibiting pleasure and desire and then judge and segregate those who cannot and will not comply. This is the key of how it could happen that people lost their individuality and became robotized—long before the beginning of the computer age. The monastery schools and forced alphabetization did their part in the brutal mind-washing process that deprived masses of people of their identity during the last millennium. The very notion of *offending* comes from witch hunt times and it is no wonder that those masses of neo witch hunters today use it again.

Abusers and abused are sitting in the same boat and they are caught in the same trap. That is why healing for both groups is very similar in that it must deal with the same scars. These scars are neither physical, nor sexual, nor emotional in the first place. They are related to the problem of *accepting self* and the sometimes karmic inability to live one's power and natural aggressiveness in a way that is positive and integrative.

To love the abused and hate the abusers is a common dichotomy that originates in a lack of understanding of the complexities of love and abuse; it's a sign of helplessness and a sentimental cover-up of the true roots of abuse.

The present situation breeds frigid powerless women from the cradle since no father can enter any more freely in a natural erotic exchange with his daughter in order to mirror her the thrill of her early womanhood. What moralistic child rearing brings about is death, not life, cripples, not powerful humans and ill responsive citizens instead of sanely and sexually responsive ones.

The present abuse paradigm and the masses of people it attracts as its believers and worshippers is the most deplorable, the most powerless and the most self-alienated form of human togetherness that I have ever seen in human social interaction. It is the prolonged kindergarten of the worst sort, the *good boy, good girl* paradigm extended into adulthood, the paradigm that paradoxically, by its very perversity, has contributed to bring about abuse in the first place.

The core message I get from most people who publicly spread their abuse story is not very different from what was formerly called *confessions*, with the difference only that the *priest* has been replaced by the *psychiatrist* and the expression *sin* by the expression *abuse*.

The Church punished the victim for having let it happen, the modern culture punishes the victim for not being aggressive enough to defend herself. Accordingly, the Church admonished sinners to comply with Church morals and thus to repress sexuality; the modern culture admonishes victims to get into therapy to boost up their aggressiveness—in order to comply to modern society's paradigm of *violence is better than sex.*

Thus, essentially, nothing has changed. It is often the punishment or the therapy more than the initial abuse that produces the guilt that erodes self-esteem. However, society's hypocrisy and the pinkish foam of sentimentality as well as the black mask of panic and mass hysteria that surrounds this whole subject renders it almost impossible to leave *what happened how it happened*—without making it up, sensationalizing it and thereby distorting and even falsifying it in the most absurd way.

It's shame and taboo, restrictions of speech and dishonesty among close relatives that prepare the ground for abuse, not openness, honesty and outspoken needs and desires.

It is a fact that if a father is socially or morally prohibited from expressing his incestuous needs *verbally* that prepares for acting out incest. The secret of harmony is naturalness and communication. If you want to perpetuate war and destruction and the sentimentality that covers up the vital facts about the true reasons of abuse, do exactly that: prevent children from fulfilling their emotional needs, and prevent both parents and children from what the late child therapist Françoise Dolto called *parler désir (to talk desire)*. For truth is dynamite in a truthless culture where the mute, blind and deaf are both the leaders and the followers, characterized by their abhorrent ignorance of life and essential life functions.

There is a larger imbeddedness needed for victimization as a social paradigm being functional as it is, in today's postmodern international consumer culture. What is needed is institutionalization, organization, structure. One chaotic soul will not do much harm as an activist, but when a whole society, by its commercial setup, sets in place huge funding for creating an abuse-centered industry, then we are facing a paradigm shift for the worse. Then we are facing a return of tyranny, of persecution, and of mass indoctrination, that we thought we could bury in our history books.

Not so. The hero culture asks for a high price. The gods of patriarchy are blood-thirstier than their matriarchal predecessors, they are highly judgmental, revengeful and fanatic, and they hate one thing more than all: *permissiveness.*

That is why the child, and childhood are in their constant focus. For it's a deadly sin in their eyes to raise children permissively, and that is why, in turn, why they need abuse to happen.

Abuse is exactly the price we pay when we deny to be permissive, and when we arrogate ourselves to be righteous demi-gods. Patriarchy is setup in a way that abuse will almost invariably happen, and that is why it creates *victims,* as a matter of logic.

Chapter Three

The Institutionalized Victim

Women in our culture are expected and encouraged to be helpless. They are supposed to play the role of the eternal victim. This is already an old rime in patriarchal culture and society, but it has been revived in the run of the child-abuse hysteria, for within the abuse culture, the single woman with one or two children has been given increased attention.

Among these women who have all in common that they share an abuse story, are many activists. Some of them are torn up by jealousy and hate against an abusive ex-husband, some revolt against discrimination at work, and some have been abused by their brothers or father, even though coming from well-to-do families.

Instead of validating abuse as a *symptom* for an underlying social disease to be detected and healed, they seem to take the symptom for the disease and choose to fight on a social or community level. And instead of turning inside in order to put a handle on their abuse story, seek out therapy, or try to see the karmic or spiritual implications of victimization, they go out to make the world save for good order, justice, righteousness and moral values. So it appears that their activism serves as a *compensation* or *ersatz* for the work on integrating their emotions that they, consciously or not, refuse to engage in. They call themselves *activists for peace* but what they are in fact is *activists of war*, and mental terrorists in their messing up and sabotaging life and love, creating paranoia by instilling in people the dreadful fear they themselves cannot handle. In fact, they are the most irresponsible of humans despite their talking about *responsibility* in every second sentence they voice; they are irresponsible because of their denial to take life for what it is: a *journey of discovery* that needs a basic amount of freedom to be lived creatively.

The group of abuse victims is the ideal breeding lot for child protectors. Considering the hangups they are suffering from, it is not astonishing to see that they are unable to accept their humanness and therefore will ultimately be unable to realize their humanity. This is truly a sad and fatal outcome because these women deserve to be healed, and they deserve to be respected in the first place. And they deserve to be listened to, and taken serious. The scars of abuse are real, and I am not here to downplay this in any way.

What I am saying is that the concern about abuse is not real in an abuse-centered culture, but a fake concern. The result is that those who have suffered abuse are not really taken serious, are not really listened to. The problem is, and this is a problem for men in just the same way, that when abuse is not healed, one or the other destructive behavior pattern may begin to swamp the personality, and as a result, you see an otherwise loving and well-balanced person transform into a hate-ridden persecutor.

These personal problems are aggravated because of the social imbeddedness of abuse. The present hero culture seems to validate women and children only in their quality as *ideal victims*.

The fact that women and children possess a genuine personality and their own right of existence is an argument relegated to *feminism*, and by doing so, to randomness. It has to be seen that our traditional Judeo-Christian culture classifies women's rights as *derived* from the adult male as the primary power holder. The Hero-Yahweh culture postulates that the primal boss, *Gee-Oh-Dee Yahweh*, created the female as a *derivative* of the male's body, a feat that contradicts all and every other creation myths as shown by an eminent expert on the matter, Joseph Campbell.

And almost as an antithesis to their being invalidated as women because of patriarchal denial, they have managed to be recognized and even institutionalized within the present abuse culture *in their quality as victims*. Generous governmental and non-governmental funding created the places, the forums, the publishing media and the institutions for them, the platforms for their activism, for realizing their fight, for acting out their hate campaigns, following the old Biblical *eye-for-eye*.

The abuse culture actively helped them create their fear-and-hate religion, their churches and lavish forums for preaching their cause of revenge, for ejaculating their poison into the vulnerable belly of an open society. And the media have helped them since the media are funded by them and because the media avidly lick their fingers to get more of sordid public wars and campaigns that ensure high sales within a huge public that lusts for *perversity*, in just the same way as the masses some centuries ago liked to attend public chastisements, hangings and torture. The abuse culture knows to manipulate public opinion so as to create still more hate, still more disgust, still more revolt, killing any voice that tries to conciliate, to bring peace, to bring love and understanding in the hate discussion. Another point to consider is the obvious parallel of treating abuse with how society generally treats disease. As a matter of fact, the *mainstream* Western medical system generally does not empower the patient to collaborate in treating disease; instead the patient is considered a victim and disease considered a more or less inevitable fate that can befall everybody. However, alternative medicine, and especially energy medicine start from a totally different point of view in that they empower the patient to actively participate in the cure.

—See, for example, Donna Eden & David Feinstein, Energy Medicine (1998).

The authors write:

> People who are suffering and experiencing themselves as victims of their own body become empowered when they are able to direct subtle energies to effect their healing.

In the same way a person who considers herself a victim of disease, the woman who thinks she will be eternally marked with a stamp because she once has been abused will end up in depression, and be dominated by alternating feelings of revolt, revenge and powerlessness. The questions I will try to answer here are what these women allegedly are fighting for versus what they are really fighting for, what they want to achieve with their fight, and what their fight really brings about, what it is that their fight covers up, and if there are perhaps karmic roots of abuse?

Let's see if we can disentangle what they *think* they are fighting for from what they are *really* fighting for.

They *think* they are fighting for a better society, a better world where there is more justice for women and girls, where men are more respectful and tender, where females are not any more subjected to humiliation and abuse but regarded in their own right, as persons with an equal standing, employed and paid according to their true capabilities, and not as second hand creatures. A world where women can fully display their creativity and their uniqueness on the public scene, where love is no more a one-sided game with *males as winners* and *females as losers*. A society that not only in its joyful Constitution but in *real life* respects women and girls as what they really are: divine creatures who need to be loved and valued.

They are *really* fighting for having the opportunity to exteriorize their terrible inner tension, to compensate for their feelings of powerlessness and self-accusation, for acting counter to their constant guilt and their low self-esteem that make it so difficult for them to find loving partners, to release part of their pent-up sexual tension through working with a kind of frenzy and for the *good cause*.

They are *really* fighting for showing to their children what they are truly able to, what they can *achieve*, to what extent their action can move and mobilize people, and for showing to themselves that they are more than pretty little girl for big daddy; they are fighting to take revenge with all men they encounter, and be it that they not always are right in this fight, which does not really damage anybody since *somewhere, somehow all men are the culprits—* in their eyes.

Against whom are they fighting? They *think* they are fighting against evil, and first of all evil men, men who abuse, who are violent and who disrespect the female.

Against whom are they *really* fighting? Against *themselves* as the silent accomplices that did not dare, or did not choose to say *no* to what they *now* consider to be a crime and a humiliation. Against those they really like to take revenge with, their abusive fathers, brothers, uncles or divorced husbands the subconscious image of whom they project on every perpetrator they now search out and persecute as a scapegoat for their own private cause that has not been solved and absolved.

What is it they want to achieve with their fight and what is it that their fight *really* produces? They want to force justice onto the world, having experienced injustice, having lost any belief in a supernatural force that is just and good and, worse, any insight that this force is actually *within* them and can be *activated* through love and forgiveness. They strangely ignore the fact that this force cannot be activated through hate and violence. Thus what their fight *really* produces is to gradually eliminate every bit of love out of their lives and, through their hateful and violent actions, out of the world at large. Through the Draconian justice they are out to inflict upon those they hate and despise, without being aware that they, having been abused and victimized, in turn abuse and victimize, applying the old rule *What has been done to me I do onto others*, they perpetuate evil in the world rather than diminishing it, they perpetuate fear, suspicion and persecution and thus insecurity, instead of acting in the world in a way to make it more secure and more peaceful. Thus, seen from a perspective other than their own, what they achieve is exactly the contrary of what they want to achieve.

What is it, then, that their fight hides? What their fight conceals are *needs*, their own unfulfilled needs and the needs of those they attack. Let's see what those needs are and if they are very different. What they need is to be loved and share love with others. This basic human need they share with those they attack.

Those who have fallen in the trap of abuse and became abusers have failed to cope with their need for love, have chosen a way of doing that was highly if not paradoxically *inappropriate* to fulfill this need—with one word: they were unable to *communicate*. And instead of communicating their need, they were communicating the violence that was the result of the repression of their need.

They are lost in their fight since those who abused them have never communicated their need, but their violence; in fact, those men who mistreated them have most probably not stretched out their hand and asked for forgiveness and have not opened themselves up to receive forgiveness, to show their vulnerability in front of the person they victimized.

So they feel truly stuck, lost in their miserable memories and their damaged self-worth, feeling dirty or ugly, not knowing that the shame is not their own but the shame of the person who abused them and that they have taken over without knowing. What all their fight is supposed to cover is nothing *but that shame*. However, it appears that this shame cannot be silenced nor diminished through terrorizing others, but through self-love and embracing our needs. It can only diminish to the extent they begin to love themselves *despite all*, and find out what exactly their needs are so that they can start exploring ways to fulfill them. The first obstacle on this way is *forgiveness*. Forgiveness is a shortcut for cases in which the one who hurt us does not stretch out his arm to ask for forgiveness because they are too proud or too shameful to do it. So we forgive them nonetheless. What happens next? The shame disappears. Why? It was *not our shame*, it was the shame we overtook from the abuser.

Through forgiving, we release another from his shame and, as a result, ourselves. What happens next? We open up to love and being loved again.

Life gratifies those who forgive because they help life in its eternal healing process, and thereby become resourceful in being creative and *pro-life.*

Life rewards their proactive stance by granting them new opportunities for love, as they have gained understanding in the human cause as a total process of existence. They have seen that life is not *should be* or *ought to*, not white or black but all shades of gray. Then, with this truly humane wisdom, they can go out and fight, and their fight will have a different quality and it will bring love, not hate, understanding and not intolerance, forgiveness and not eye-for-eye. Then, they might also understand that everything is cyclic and that abuse can have karmic reasons, too. As a result of their inner transformation, they may well go out and change the laws and will then perhaps be ready to see abusers with their needs and their good intentions and they could both communicate about the cases that are *not* clear-cut. Then they could see and reason out *other options*, after having clearly seen the *needs on both sides*, regardless of the law and social mores, but for the sake of love and the beauty of it all. Then, what would happen is that the former institutionalized victims would begin to be useful and effective collaborators for the *common good* since they eventually gained real knowledge, which is self-knowledge, and experience instead of accumulating theories, and by turning away from the path of revenge, they have gained humility and real understanding of the human condition in its totality.

So why don't they get on this track?

They would need to make a firm and lucid decision first and seek out *healing themselves* instead of searching for healing evil *in the world*, and in others. Their focus is wrong because they are as sick as the collective in which they were born. *Collective psychosis* is not the fruit of a soundly adjusted mindset. Paracelsus said that you are always wrong when you are sick. He meant that there is intelligence in the body that reacts sensitively to maladjustments in the psyche with the result that physical sickness often indicates a mental or emotional disturbance.

Thus a society that is sick can only be wrong; a society where seventy percent of the population are depressive and take some kind of drug to keep going is so sick that its value judgments *cannot seriously be taken into account* by a scientifically minded and lucid individual. It would be foolish and against any logic to assume that a society that in its majority lives wrongly should exceptionally be right in their views about sexuality or love. It is much more sound to argue that a society that disregards life to a point that it can bring about the nuclear overkill thousands of times with its accumulated weapons is one that is ignorant about life and the intrinsic quality of living; and a society that is brilliant in inventing devices how to kill more effectively and then hypocritely preaches the *love of the neighbor* has disqualified itself from the start.

If we had asked Lao-tzu about abuse he would most probably have answered that there are many desires in the human being and that some of them come about through our early experiences, some of them through karmic memories and some because of our ambitions for the future. And he would have concluded that while the etiology may be one or the other, the important in life is that we value the experience as it was.

This means to live with what we got instead of judging life, judging the creator force and thus spreading *stupidity for sale*. For such a point of view, which sadly enough is the point of view of the majority today in most high-tech countries, is truly schizophrenic. The surface of a vinyl record may be scratched while the record is played. The music, if we are honest, is part of the scratching yet it is by far prevailing over the noise that the scratching produces.

But what society says is that it is no music at all. And this is a lie—no way! A paranoid society produces paranoid judgments. In order to keep its system safe, it *must* proceed that way. A paranoid judgment is one that is produced by irrational motives, especially by fear, and other factors that distort perception. The problem is that people who are complying uncritically with society's paranoid rules on that matter are more or less locked in an irrational mindset and thus ward off any rational arguments.

And their paranoid track can be identified by their typical behavior to justify their rampant irrationality with pseudo-rational arguments, while thinking of themselves being rational-minded people. In fact, they are lesser rational and also lesser responsible than their lesser mature children ever could be. As a result, and as it were with striking logic, they cannot be said to be valid protectors of their children.

They cannot protect because they themselves are not safe. *Quid est demonstrandum.*

Chapter Four

The Hidden Swine

What fathers and other lovers have in common in an abuse-centered culture is that they are potential child molesters. The very fact that a man and a child go together to a rest room signifies, within the paranoid culture, the immediate danger of *child sexual assault.*

The abuse culture seems to suspect a hidden swine in every man, a swine that is easily enticed into criminal acts by external stimuli. Typically such enticement is triggered by undressed children who, by their vulnerability, unconsciously push the otherwise socially adapted adult into asocial acts. In most child care centers all over the Western industrialized world, it is now the stern rule for male day care workers to be accompanied by a female worker when they bring a child to the toilet. It seems strange that in a male-dominated culture the male has been depreciated to such extent.

The main reasons for this phenomenon are seen by some in the emancipation of women. Especially within the pedophile literature, feminism is frowned upon as the social culprit for the depreciation of men in early child education. But I think this argument is based on a perception error. The male has not been depreciated in our culture, and feminism cannot be said to per se depreciate the male.

The answer is that men who work in day care are not defined, by this culture, *as males*. They fall outside of the social frame. They are not defined as females either. They are considered a perverted form of males, something like *childmen*. In fact, in the sweat-and-hit culture that modern consumer society originates from, the male was traditionally far from the children, a hunter. A man interested in his children, in a physical or affectionate sense, was a rare exception. This type of men that are still today the molding image for many men are brute, harsh, rough, smelly and intellectually mediocre. With the development of technology, when technical knowledge and complex education were becoming a must, this old male role model began to change, but it did not lead to a full integration of *intellectuals* within the hero paradigm.

The hero mindset favors *action, roughness and brutality*, an attitude of the male where deed comes before thought and where feelings are either choked or serve a well-defined purpose: family, procreation, survival. The typical face expressions and other body language displayed in most modern television series show this evidently when you look at the *Gestalt* of the behavior of the hero.

The male hero typically has a blown-up chest, a large stiff neck and highly contracted face muscles. His language is crude, short, reductionist and aggressive, reminding more the barking of a dog than the eloquence of a soul-being. His actions are cunning, not wise, just, not philanthropic, efficient, not integrated. His emotions are disconnected from his intellect and are *purposeful.* Emotions just for feeling good, for sharing, for being spontaneous and joyful are depreciated as childish, unmanly or superficial.

In older civilizations this was different and still is quite different in those that have survived until this day. In traditional cultures, we find an *intelligentsia* from times immemorial that has had an impact on society and on the formation of its value system. The image of the male in those older cultures is different from the image of the typical modern male. The traditional value system in cultures that are closer to nature and that have a long tradition tolerates feminine attributes in a man with much more ease. Also in terms of erotic attractiveness, the image of the male is more of the homely partner type, instead of the outdoor kind of guy. The prototype image of the good male is the family-lover who also cares for the children, and the man that possesses some kind of *emotional intelligence* and can bond with the female also on an intuitive level.

Often, this image of the male in older civilizations is complemented by social permissiveness regarding mistress keeping, and the recognition, socially and even legally, of non-married couples. In many of these old civilizations, be it in Europe, or the traditional cultures of Persia, Egypt, Japan or China, mistress keeping was a tradition since centuries and is not really contested by the female emancipation movements. What the more traditional woman desires in a man is trust, care and responsibility, and if a man manages to have a mistress but still can be trusted and cares for his wife and children, and if he is tactful and discrete enough not to bring shame to his neighborhood through his double marriage, most marriages and family reputation can go undamaged even over years.

In modern culture's hero paradigm, the *hidden swine* image creates havoc. It is not the male in the original sense defined by the patriarchal paradigm that is regarded with suspicion, but the *childman*, or what is regarded as such: the man that cannot be subsumed under the tight rules that the hero paradigm holds for men. The *childman* is a man who is considered childish, infantile, lacking emotional growth. In reality, things look different and the *childman* myth is a typical *compensation archetype* in the Jungian sense, fed by the psychic energy of *projection.*

—A compensation archetype is not a real archetype in the Jungian sense but one that compensates for a projection. When we repress any information from our conscious memory surface, psychology found that we tend to project this repressed content on others. Thus, instead of sweeping in front of our own door, we begin to see evil in others. The evil we see is the energy our own disowned selves. On the level of archetypes, this process is similar. When we repress to render a certain archetype conscious, and try to wipe it from our memory surface, a fictive artificial archetype is created that replaces the repressed archetype and that is often a caricature of the original one, and really grotesque. Historical example is the goat archetype as a symbol for the raw male sexual power that was repressed by early Christianity, and the result was the devil, as a compensation archetype that typically is depicted in old scriptures as a goat, or that is goat-like in appearance.

Projection is a psychic automatism that is a by-product of repression. When an emotion or desire gets repressed, projection sets in and what is blinded out from wake consciousness is projected upon others—who then get the blame for what is originally a part of the person's own life.

The myth here clashes with reality because this kind of men are generally rather sensitive and intelligent, a lot more sensitive and intelligent than the prototype that defines the culture; and again contrary to the social hero, he has a healthy focus upon the family, indoor activities, females, children and pets. He has a lesser hunting instinct but a much stronger caring instinct than his mainstream counterpart. In both the child care setting and in the family, such men, instead of being appreciated, rather are regarded with suspicion: they are suspected to step over the line once in a while to abuse of the closeness they have to the children for arriving at a one-sided, ego-tripped form of ripped-off sexual *gain.*

The main assumption that is contained in this modern-day collective fantasy is that the normal male *is not and has not to be* close to children. If we penetrate into the logic of this argument, we quickly see where the ghost is coming from. It's the fear of *closeness* as such, the fear of *emotions*, of *feelings* that is at the root of this paradigm. It's Puritanism at its best. Puritanism is not primarily a sex repression but a *repression of feelings!* The repression of sex is a consequence of the repression of feelings, of emotions and emotionality, not the other way around as most people tend to think.

Psychological research has shown that the reality is pretty much contrary to these collective myths. The man who is closer to his feelings and, as a result, closer to females and to children, has proven to show more responsibility and has a *rather low abuse profile* while the man who is the typical male of the hero paradigm, who is disconnected from his feelings and far from his family and children, is generally less responsible and has a *rather high abuse profile.*

—See, for example, Lauretta Bender & Abram Blau, The Reaction of Children to Sexual Relations with Adults, American J. Orthopsychiatry 7 (1937), 500-518, Brant & Tisza, The Sexually Misused Child, American J. Orthopsychiatry,

47(1)(1977), Groth, A. Nicholas, Men Who Rape: The Psychology of the Offender, New York: Perseus Publishing, 1980, Colin Pritchard, The Child Abusers, New York: Open University Press, 2004, Christopher Bagley, Child Abusers: Research and Treatment, New York: Universal Publishers, 2003, Assessing Dangerousness: Violence by Sexual Offenders, Batterers and Child Abusers, New York: Sage Publications, 2004.

The above-mentioned legislation is made by the majority of men and women who follow the mainstream paradigm. Through this legislation, the hidden swine myth is *projected* on men who are, as a fact, less abusive and more integrated, more adapted to the challenges of our times than the stereotype male who is at pains with accepting shared responsibility in the couple and a society in which the female is gaining more equality.

Thus, it can be said that this legislation, as so many now taken in matters of 'public morals,' is not only archaic but simply nonsense. History and psychological research in hindsight will show that those who are going to be trapped by this legislation and prove to be *hidden swines* will be not the *childmen*, but the very heroes and mainstream stereotype males, not the contemplative type of men, but the persecutor kind of guys, not those who openly confess and express their *pedoemotions*, but those who repress them and plague the media and political agendas with their flatulent constipated bowels.

—I define Pedoemotions as a universal erotic base attraction that nature has built in adult men and women toward children so as to ensure their loving care for the young. This base attraction however does not generally become sexualized, but is well acted out through tactile closeness with the (naked) child. In certain cases, this base attraction can become eroticized, which may result in the feeling of sexual attraction of an adult toward a child, which may, or not be acted out. Research has brought to daylight that, however, in most cases, such attraction is not acted out by actual sexual penetration of the child, but rather by fondling, shared nakedness and masturbatory acts. See, for example, Bender Lauretta & Blau, Abram, The Reaction of Children to Sexual Relations with Adults, American J. Orthopsychiatry 7 (1937), 500-518, Brant & Tisza, The Sexually Misused Child, American J. Orthopsychiatry, 47(1)(1977).

Chapter Five

Street Monster

Monster Culture is an expression I have forged to describe a state of mind or mindset that is deeply ingrained in negativity and basically distorted regarding the values that life fosters, a paradigm that is primarily morality-centered.

The typical behavior of people with this mindset is that they are lurking at every corner for detecting and reporting illegal or *obscene* behavior.

These people are unaware of the fact that the way they look at life and at relationships is by itself obscene because it is deeply distorted by a life-denying and hateful morality paradigm that situates nature outside of man's realm of life or, with other words, that considers creation as consisting of a good, decent part and a bad, indecent part. The Puritan worldview that is an intrinsic part of this mindset forbids namely to consider natural emotions to be situated on the good or divine side of the human being. As a result, a schizoid split of the human soul must by definition occur within this mindset. What is fundamentally disturbing in the present discussion of so-called abuse is that humans in leading positions try to smash an open debate, caring little about constitutional rights or integral principles of democratic human togetherness such as free speech.

The effect of the fear that is created by enormous— and enormously expensive—national, supranational and international witch hunts is that almost every rational and unprejudiced discussion about intergenerational love has disappeared from the media world during about the last decade.

There is power in our difference and we smash this power in our attempt to comply with life models we want to *imitate* for security reasons, for mere comfort, for mere safety—or for justifying a particular worldview in view of a majority that is hostile toward it.

In the beginning there is fear; and this fear can become overwhelming. The fear is not, however, a signal of mental illness, but a necessary phenomenon that accompanies the birth of one's own reality. This process can be gradual and it can be sudden. The more sudden it is, the more fear will be experienced. Fear is a strong indicator that a process of *individuation* has been initiated in one's life. This really marks the life of all true heroes, of all geniuses, of all those that we admire because they made or make a difference in the world.

They *all* had to go through that. It is from this point of observation that further down the road of my research I began to wonder why the abuse culture worships brute insensitive monster-heroes that are actually prototypes of abusers, instead of projecting the image of the sensitive, educated, humane and intelligent male?

The *Monster Culture* fosters a worldview that fundamentally denies tenderness. It is an essentially immature paradigm of people who have no idea of the *sensual-sexual* and *erotically intelligent* dimension of living, of the evolutionary experience of mating for the sake of shared joy, and of the need for the human soul to grow through loving encounters. It's a worldview of frigid women and impotent men who are sadistic enough to institutionalize through their collective paranoia *the systematic emotional and tactile deprivation of children* which is, after all, a new form of institutionalized child abuse. While the right approach to counter abuse would be to foster a worldview that allows emotions and that is sympathetic to *emotional intelligence*, healthy touch, and natural cooperation between males and females in child rearing.

It can be argued that withholding body touch in child rearing as an ingredient of nurturant tactile stimulation under the header of 'preventing child abuse' represents a cultural depravation. We can actually identify here a cultural pattern that consists of two elements: *deprivation* and *depravation*.

Deprivation is inflicted upon the young with the intention of keeping intact the cultural ideal of *morality*. Let me give an example. In olden times, when there was little care bestowed upon orphans, the only caretakers of orphans used to be priests or monks. This tradition was especially fostered by the Christian religion. Part of this tradition, that was still alive in the Renaissance, and that even has survived in provincial regions in Italy and other Catholic

Mediterranean countries was that infants born out of wedlock or infants born as a result of rape, maimed infants or any other unwanted infants could be deposited in a hole in the monastery's wall. Typically, when the child was a boy, the mother could leave him with the monks, when it was a girl, with the nuns. Else, there were certain dedicated spots under trees around certain monasteries where babies could be dropped in order to prevent them from being drowned or otherwise murdered. These children who were brought up by monks and nuns were destined for serving the monastery later on, as monks or nuns.

Now, while I do not doubt that generally monks and nuns tried to give these orphans love and care, there is one essential thing that was from the start excluded in this kind of tutelary relationships: *tactile stimulation*. As the morality code of the Church labeled any form of nudity as sinful, it was unthinkable in such institutions that, for example, orphans could share the bathtub with a caretaker or with other children, or that they could experience tactile pleasure while sleeping together naked. For the puzzled reader, I want to make sure that I am not misunderstood here.

I am obviously not talking about *sex*, and I am not talking about any other form of the caretaker being out for emotional or sexual *gratification*. I am talking here about the most basic and essential form of caretaking there is: giving the child abundant tactile stimulation.

In my view, to deny children sensual touch and experience is a form of depravation. Here the child's best is sacrificed to a cultural standard that was established not for the best of children, but for the best of *morality*—whatever that really *is*.

That such specific depravation can lead to psychological distress, namely, depression, is an insight we gained from psychoneuroimmunology, neurology, psychoanalysis and child psychology, an insight that centuries ago a monk or nun could only have intuitively, if ever. Thus, when a monk or nun acted against the taboo of *sensual body touch*, the result would have been strong guilt, shame and fear. I argue that letting fear pervert one's 'life paradigm' to a point to deny a child healthy body contact is a form of depravement.

My point is that this argument can be extrapolated to the whole of today's *child-abuse* debate. It's a form of depravement to collectively mess up and mix up natural love and healthy body touch with abuse and harm. It's a cultural madness altogether.

The strategy of mechanistic science was mainly focused upon rationalizing irrational thought patterns around the greater issues of life, love, emotions and sexuality. After some twenty or more years of such strategy, we can attempt to have a look at the results.

What we see is something like a disaster! The admittedly very informative, very well-balanced and very rational strategy of hyper-rational science had a very limited impact on a very limited circle of intellectuals; it has not reached an even slight percentage of the mass culture.

Why? Well, the ordinary human is primarily driven by emotions and not very interested in browsing scientific *readers* and information bulletins of certain scientific disciplines. It's common knowledge today that the mass media, in the meantime, are totally closed to any kind of balanced controversial discussion that goes beyond the daily whitewash—or rather, *blackwash*. Some attribute the present flight back into the Middle-Ages to a *New Age of Fascism* to come.

I rather believe that the culprit here was Cartesian science. That science tried to wipe emotional content under the carpet, arguing that because the majority was anyway hopelessly emotional and irrational, science had to be *extremely rational*. Yet the world is not black and white. And it's not divided and dividable into *rational versus irrational*. It's not clear-cut. To depict people with a naturally critical mind as something like street monsters shows not only the pitifully brainless condition of most media consumers today, but it demonstrates the *helplessness* of a society in front of *erotic intelligence*.

We could learn a lesson by considering why, by contrast, repressive and abusive governments are generally successful in subduing masses of people under the pseudo-protective umbrella of their regimes. It is because those governments tend to be highly *emotional, irrational and very little intellectual*. Thus, the basis of the population is attracted toward their message even though they may know that the people behind the screens are nothing but mafia in uniform. It is because those at the top come actually from the same social layer as those at the bottom, and because they have some basic expressions in common. Typically, the way they tend to see the world is the dichotomy of winning-or-losing, a basically option-deprived worldview.

Society needs the myth of the *street monster* in order to hide this truth since the revelation of the secret would be very disturbing.

The present blind-folding educational system with its inhuman repression of emotions would work no more. Even to a much lesser degree, if only the young generations got a true understanding of the mechanism of emotional repression and the real motivations behind this repression, the present order could no more be maintained. There would be revolt, on every level, in every institution, school or university, in every social organization. There would be organized, systematic revolt and terror-against-terror, there would be open fight and perhaps civil war. Yet we do not live in a democratic culture, but in a *primal horde*. The human being, despite being a *zoon politicon*, never developed true *democracy*.

In a *primal horde*, those only are taken serious socially and politically who have power and who have achieved to value and love themselves with a certain feeling of pride or a positive sort of narcissism that they project onto the group. It's the monkey who beats his chest in victory. That's the state of consciousness of that *primal horde* that our society represents. It's literally a monkey mentality.

CHAPTER SIX

The Goddess Within

It is elucidating to observe the complex interaction of the individual with the group in Judeo-Christian culture. It cannot be mere chance that the present Western societies are the most repressive regarding emotions and *erotic intelligence*.

Joseph Campbell explains that the Goddess was killed in the violent hunter societies that preceded our Judeo-Christian culture.

—A goddess is a female deity by contrast to a male deity known as God. Many cultures have goddesses, sometimes alone, but more often as part of a larger pantheon that includes both the conventional genders and in some cases even hermaphrodite deities. As the concept of monotheism and polytheism is relativistic, so the related concepts of god and goddess can be culturally misunderstood. Gender identity applied to a god and goddess may veil deeper tendencies of patriarchy and matriarchy, which may to have equivalence to the rift between monotheism and polytheism.

This *murder of the Goddess* is explicated in the Bible; it is not a myth but a historical and psychological fact.

The murder of the Goddess was an early castration of the female part of our libido and the value that, in our unconscious mind, is associated with the *yin* force or energy in us.

> —Freud's libido concept is controversial, today more than ever before, because early writings suggest that Freud originally meant libido to be a specific bioplasmatic energy in the organism that could be compared to what Reich later discovered as the orgone, but in later writings, Freud seemed to distance himself from this concept and consider libido simply as synonymous with sexual drive or pleasure function.

> The concepts of yin and yang originate in ancient Chinese philosophy and metaphysics, which describes two primal opposing but complementary forces found in all things in the universe

It seems that this castration has taken place also in other cultures such as the Confucian culture. The *I Ching* oracle book, despite its subtle truth that the yin and yang alternation of energies is beneficial and that the two energies are mutually supportive and complementary, is not as subtle, but rather outspoken and openly judgmental as to the beneficial or harmful effects of the *yin*. It estranges that in the *I Ching* the *yin* energy is generally the bad force while *yang* energy is generally the good one.

I study the I Ching for now almost twenty years, but I have not found an explanation for this obvious predilection of the wisdom book for the *yang* energy to the detriment of the *yin* energy.

—See Peter Fritz Walter, The Leadership I Ching: Your Daily Companion for Practical Guidance, 4th Edition, 2018.

I could well imagine that the hexagrams where this is expressed were falsified by Confucian scholars, as we know that the I Ching is of course much older than Confucianism, and that it originally did not contain that Puritan touch and the sexist bias it got from Confucian sources.

Confucianism and Platonism have in common that they erected *male hubris* into a historical and philosophical paradigm that survived until these days and that is at the basis of the actual misbalance of our psychological and social setup and the oppression of the female and female wisdom. It is also at the root of our present moralistic setup of social values. It is a rigid, intellectual, and mechanistic paradigm of *fixed values* that tries to control life instead of yielding to the steady flow of positive and negative, creative and destructive forces and energies that compose and perpetuate life. It is a paradigm that tries to comprehend life through *thought* and not through intuition.

The opposite paradigm, that has respected and valued the *Goddess Within*, has been forwarded by *Heraclites of Ephesus (535-475 BC)* in the West and by *Lao-tzu (604-531 BC)* in the East. This paradigm is based upon the integration of opposing values or forces and not upon their antagonism. It does not divide creation into *good versus bad*, but starts from a general acceptance of all-that-is. It is the paradigm that naturally accepts the female as equal to the male since it values the *yin* and *yang* energies as complementary forces that reinforce and rejuvenate each other.

It is obvious that both the Platonic and Confucian life philosophies breed antagonism and violence, whereas the intelligent philosophies of Heraclites in the West, and Lao-tzu in the East purport a flexible form of peace that rolls and flows with life instead of obstructing vital energies through rigid either-or, good-or-bad judgments that hinder any comprehension of the intrinsic quality of life's dynamic manifestation.

Love manifests through *energy*; energy is consciousness, and every attempt to imprison it in intellectual, mental and moralistic frameworks of rigid antagonistic values will only damage it. Much of the present one-sided and confused abuse discussion comes from this mindset of male hubris that is in last resort a cultural hubris, a racial hubris and a paradigmatic hubris.

This is why, through truly understanding human love, we can come to understand why this present society is sick in its very roots, alienated from its true source which is the moving, loving and creating *energy of the universe*, the cosmic breath, ether, ch'i or *prana*.

Chapter Seven

Emotional Child Abuse

The much more important problem in the context of abuse is *emotional abuse*, since it is devastating yet it is hardly ever discussed or researched upon. And in the public abuse discussion, it is completely left out. Significantly so, in my rather large bibliography, there is only one single publication to be found on emotional child abuse. This is so because I simply only found one single book on the matter, which is after all scandalous in view of the importance of the problem.

I was myself only vaguely aware of this issue when, during my law and music studies in the United States, I was made aware of it by a sixteen-year old girl, the daughter of a university professor. She was only sixteen but looked like a grown woman. However she was treated, by the whole family, like a baby. The mother was a rigid, neurotic and moralistic dread of the worst sort that stiffened every conversation through her hostile regard and lifeless cynical remarks.

One day mother decided that the girl had to take piano lessons with me. No question was asked if she was ever *interested* in it in the first place. Her younger brother was playing violin against his will, and he did fairly good, so it was reasoned by their Chinese mother that the girl had to play an instrument as well. And now the opportunity was there with the *nice student* from abroad, and that chance was not going to be wasted.

I tried. The girl came and we spent a few lessons talking about her family. She did not do any exercises and not even cut her fingernails. She could not play one single measure without mistakes. I gave up because I found it *foul* to play a participating role in this sordid game that tracked the girl into something she absolutely did not want. Once she cried and I desperately consoled her, learning that she had wanted to go to a rock concert in town which however she was denied by her parents with the argument that the *obscene texts* of the songs could *hurt her*. I stopped the lessons with her.

The evening before my departure back to Europe, I was invited to their house for dinner. After the dinner, I went to say good bye to the girl, and she immediately came to the door and took me by the hand, pulling me into a kind of dressing area in a more protected back part of her room. Then she began talking vividly and with an intensity I had never before seen in her:

—I must talk to you! I wanted to tell you so much, since a long time, but I never dared to.

—What is it?

—It's about my father. I know that you write a study about child abuse and incest, right?

—Yes.

—Well, I wanted to tell you that your research is really very important, but I want to direct your attention to another form of child abuse that is perhaps not yet very well-known. It's *emotional child abuse*. Do you get what I am talking about?

—I'm not sure …

—Well, you have seen how I am treated by him. I am his baby, his sweetheart, his eternal pacifier, but I am not a person in my own right for my parents. I feel that I have no rights at all, and first of all, no right to love anybody other than them, I mean *him*. Do you see that?

—Yes, the rock concert …

—For example. That's only one of many little details.

—What can I do for you?

—You have done already much for me. I am thinking not only of myself when I request something from you …

—What?

-—To write a study about *emotional child abuse*. Sexual abuse is one thing and I think there is already much research about it. But emotional abuse is much more subtle and I find it is perhaps still more damaging because everybody finds it okay and I have *nobody* on my side, absolutely nobody.

—I see.

We were going to sit on her bed for a moment, and she cried.

—I will miss you so much, I can't tell you.

—I'll miss you too, and I promise you I'll do that research and write a study about it.

—If you do that, it's the best you can ever do for me, and so many others in my situation!

Traditionally, in our society, children, and especially female children, were the possessions of the father, and not persons in their own right. From this point of departure, it was rather the rule than the exception that children were emotionally manipulated into pleasing puppets, and the part they took to live their own life was reduced to a ridiculous façade of puppet-play, a set of childish behavior that no adult was ever taking serious.

The child was driven into being a nonsensical creature, a being without any truly significant movements, thoughts or ideas. Thus devoid of anything original, the child could be used as a container for adults' projections and, worse, a *poison container* (DeMause). It then becomes logical that these children-toys-for-their-parents deprived of anything truly of their own were to be emotionally crippled since their own appetites would clearly interfere with the parent's exclusive right to appropriate them, to incorporate them pseudo-cannibalistically, to strip them *for inspection*, to violate them for punishment and to kill them as the ultimate ratio once they were declared *useless eaters* (Lloyd DeMause).

The right of the male parent to kill his offspring still exists in many Asian and Islamic cultures and it was established at the outset of Judeo-Christian culture as the Torah, the Koran and the Bible tell us through many stories about fathers who killed their sons or daughters.

Emotional abuse is a residue of the pseudo-cannibalistic child incorporation that psychoanalysis has identified as a form of oral fixation, a hang-up in parents' own lives. What these parents actually are searching for is an illusionary amount of *emotional security* that manifests neurotically by the desire to keep their child save from the harshness of life, from imagined dangers, perverse strangers and all that hairy folk that children actually need to have around if they are to grow into a healthy awareness of reality.

Emotional abuse is *real abuse* in that the child is overpowered by the energy of the parent in a way that their own energy is smashed or invalidated.

This is in emotional abuse even more evident, in my view, than in sexual abuse because in emotional abuse children have to remain totally and deadly passive, subjected to a prison-like existence in the hands of neurotic and often compulsive parents that lead lifeless existences. Along with being shut off from the reality of life, these children are emotionally exploited by their parents in that they have no emotional life of their own, but represent live mirrors for their parents' emotions. Every time they voice an emotion of their own, they risk to be treated as *traitors* of the bond that the parents threaten to cut if the child does not stand to his or her duty as an obedient projection recipient. That is why, in conflictual situations, those parents can and do actually become very violent.

In family conversations, these children typically have to remain silent. If they voice an opinion, they are bluntly ignored or vehemently contradicted, or else accused with fostering *aberrant opinions*. In extreme cases, they are told to shut up, to *wash their mouth* or to leave the room. This happens even when they have reached adolescence and with many it continues far into adulthood, reason why later bonds with parents are often violently cut off. It happens in such families that elder parents are put in institutions where they don't stop complaining about the lacking care of their children, while nurses or psychologists who have seen the interaction they maintain with their children tend to sympathize with the children rather than with the parents.

Traditionally patriarchal societies tend to justify emotional abuse with the argument the child had to render *gratitude* to their parents and be docile and obedient. This meant, in good English, that the child had to be a good and patient listener to their parents' sorrows and concerns, and put their own concerns behind to a point to forget about them. This meant also to put the parents' emotional needs first, and to put one's own emotional needs, if they were ever recognized at all, behind.

The most flagrant extinction of children's own personality, individuality and originality is typically declared of secondary importance in front of the all-encompassing parental love and care that children had to respect and choke like an unwanted, bitter medicine *for their own good.*

Those who need to be cured, however, are not the children, but definitely the parents.

—See Alice Miller, Thou Shalt Not Be Aware: Society's Betrayal of the Child, New York: Noonday, 1998 and For Your Own Good: Hidden Cruelty in Child-Rearing and the Roots of Violence, New York: Farrar, Straus & Giroux, 1983.

CHAPTER EIGHT

Mind-Body Dilemma

Most of us have forgotten that our bodies were the first and certainly the most natural source of pleasure. Alienated from our bodies, we compensate for the lost paradise of *Being* through *Having*, possessing, consuming, to paraphrase Erich Fromm (1900-1980).

Our mind-body dilemma starts in early childhood. The progress of civilization has a high price. We pay for it with our bodies that we gradually destroy. For a body that is not connected to a soul is a *dead body*. The process of alienation that leads to this gradual decay of the human body is an integral part of the conditioning for consumer society. It begins as early as in childhood. Without the early conditioning toward toys as a body pleasure ersatz, people would not accept the later *ersatz satisfactions* they receive for the sacrifice of primary body pleasure.

> —See James W. Prescott, Body Pleasure and the Origins of Violence, Bulletin of the Atomic Scientists, 10-20 (1975) and Deprivation of Physical Affection as a Primary Process in the Development of Physical Violence: A Comparative and Cross-Cultural Perspective, in: David G. Gil, ed., Child Abuse and Violence, New York: Ams Press, 1979.

Sigmund Freud (1856-1939) thought man develops creativity through the *sublimation* of his primary sexual desire. Culture is thought to be the product of a transformation of original libido into a form of creative energy that serves cultural purposes. *But is this thesis true?*

I think that it is true and not true at the same time. It is true insofar as the prohibition and transformation of instincts leads in fact to a form of culture, an *ersatz* for the culture that would have been created through living our original instincts. And it is not true in the sense that sublimation leads to only an *ersatz culture* and not a true and original culture.

That is why I came to believe that our culture is not a culture, but a non-culture, because it is an *ersatz* culture. Ancient cultures, for example the *Minoan* culture of Crete did not grow upon the sublimation of sexual pleasure but upon its fulfillment. It seems that high human civilization can grow on the basis not of sublimation but of *real satisfaction* of sexual desires of all kinds. Minoan culture truly has been superior to our modern culture, more developed, more knowledgeable and, last not least, more *peaceful and harmonious*. The rape and destruction of this and other high cultures of Antiquity through invading patriarchal tribes was one of the turning points in human history. Turning points for culture to turn into *pig culture*. It was from this time and parallel events in other cultures that mankind took the turn into *pseudo-culture;* it was from this time that the artificial and hypocrite, the stupid and doctrinaire, the false and arrogant, together with violence, war and destruction, began to dominate the natural and naturally intelligent original cultures that preceded them. Riane Eisler spoke about the *truncation of civilization.*

> —See Riane Eisler, The Chalice and the Blade: Our history, Our future, San Francisco: Harper & Row, 1995

All leading religions absolved and baptized this turn of mankind into the false, manipulative and undemocratic *Barbarian Primal Horde* that represents present-day mainstream culture. Religions have consciously played the role of a *catalyzer* in the conditioning of man for war and destruction, although they globally pay lip service to the contrary.

For years, I have studied the culture and lifestyle of tribal peoples. And I was amazed at their wistful ways to realize our human potential, and at their unique manners of helping children learn about themselves, to acquire self-knowledge from their most tender years. It is significant that tribal cultures that put the human body and *body sensitivity* in the foreground of cultural, artistic and social life do not need to preach love. *They love.* And they do not need to heal love because they *practice* love. Their religion is not the integrity of pseudo-moralistic values, but the integrity of *love.*

Religion, in tribal cultures, is not a power factor and does not exert power over individuals. They practice the true *religio*, giving guidance to people who are searching for the truth about coming and going, transcendence of suffering, care for the sick and needy, for those who acted against the law, and the dying.

I admire the *North American Indians* for having preserved original and pure religion that was once universal for all human beings and that originated in Hawaii, as the *Huna religion*, practiced by the *kahunas*, the natives of that island.

> —The Kahunas are the natives from Hawaii and they have acquired fame and international recognition through the astounding insights their spiritual methods foster, even with Westerners. See, for example, Max 'Freedom' Long, The Secret Science at Work: The Huna Method as a Way of Life, Marina del Rey: De Vorss Publications, 1995 and Growing Into Light: A Personal Guide to Practicing the Huna Method, Marina del Rey: De Vorss Publications, 1955, as well as Erika Nau, Self-Awareness Through Huna, Virginia Beach: Donning, 1981.

A pleasure-based society will probably find violence pornographic.

When I worked with children, I saw that little children seem to be free of these value judgments, and that freely raised children are primarily pleasure-oriented. But since they have subtle antennas for the tolerance level of their adult environment, they quickly adapt to those pseudo-values, simply for avoiding the displeasure resulting from punishment and reject for non-accepted forms of conduct.

Postface

Summary

As a summary of this essay, I would like to firmly root our focus on the fact that abuse is not just an individual matter, but also a cultural problem, and even something like a cultural disease. And when this is the case, the healing of the individual affliction is not as easy as it may look at first sight.

This is so because ontogenetic and phylogenetic processes are interwoven and entangled in a rather complex way, as modern systems research has shown us.

But the main problem in the etiology of abuse, and the nasty fact that it perpetuates over generations is the infamous ideology of *victimization*.

This very slogan is a belief, and it's so powerful as a belief that it reinforces and perpetuates the belief of individuals in myths like spiritual predestination, genetic predisposition, or the above-mentioned belief that once a victim, one has to remain a victim for the rest of one's life.

> —Genetic determinism is a fundamental error of an outdated principle-ridden biology that was ignorant about the systemic properties of living systems, and only now, and gradually, is overcome by a truly ecological approach. Fritjof Capra has outlined the controversy very clearly in his various books. In The Turning Point: Science, Society And The Rising Culture, New York: Simon & Schuster (Flamingo), 1987, Capra writes on pages 289-290):
>
> 'This nonlinear interconnectedness of living organisms indicates that the conventional attempts of biomedical science to associate diseases with single causes are highly problematic. Moreover, it shows the fallacy of 'genetic determination', the belief that various physical or mental features of an individual organism are 'controlled' or 'dictated' by its genetic makeup. The systems view makes it clear that genes do not uniquely determine the functioning of an organism as cogs and wheels determine the working of a clock. Rather, genes are integral parts of an ordered whole and thus conform to its systemic organization.

When outside beliefs reinforce inner beliefs, most people will resist change and remain stuck in their rigid assumptions about life.

BIBLIOGRAPHY

ABRAMS, JEREMIAH (ED.)

RECLAIMING THE INNER CHILD
New York: Tarcher/Putnam, 1990

ALSTON, JOHN P. / TUCKER, FRANCIS

THE MYTH OF SEXUAL PERMISSIVENESS
The Journal of Sex Research, 9/1 (1973)

APPLETON, MATTHEW

A FREE RANGE CHILDHOOD
Self-Regulation at Summerhill School
Foundation for Educational Renewal, 2000

ARCAS, GÉRALD, DR

GUÉRIR LE CORPS PAR L'HYPNOSE ET L'AUTO-HYPNOSE
Paris: Sand, 1997

ARIÈS, PHILIPPE

L'ENFANT ET LA FAMILLE SOUS L'ANCIEN RÉGIME
Paris, Seuil, 1975

CENTURIES OF CHILDHOOD
New York: Vintage Books, 1962

GESCHICHTE DER KINDHEIT
Frankfurt/M: DTV, 1998

ARNTZ, WILLIAM & CHASSE, BETSY
____

WHAT THE BLEEP DO WE KNOW
20th Century Fox, 2005 (DVD)

DOWN THE RABBIT HOLE QUANTUM EDITION
20th Century Fox, 2006 (3 DVD Set)

RELATIONSHIPS AND LIFE CYCLES
Astrological Patterns of Personal Experience
Sebastopol, CA: CRCS Publications, 1993

ATLEE, TOM
____

THE TAO OF DEMOCRACY
Using Co-Intelligence to Create a World That Works for All
North Charleston, SC: Imprint Books / WorldWorks Press, 2003

BACHELARD, GASTON
____

THE POETICS OF REVERIE
Translated by Daniel Russell
Boston: Beacon Press, 1971

BIBLIOGRAPHY

Baggins, David Sadofsky

Drug Hate and the Corruption of American Justice
Santa Barbara: Praeger, 1998

Bagley, Christopher

Child Abusers
Research and Treatment
New York: Universal Publishers, 2003

Balter, Michael

The Goddess and the Bull
Catalhoyuk, An Archaeological Journey
to the Dawn of Civilization
New York: Free Press, 2006

Bandler, Richard

Get the Life You Want
The Secrets to Quick and Lasting Life Change
With Neuro-Linguistic Programming
Deerfield Beach, Fl: HCI, 2008

Barbaree, Howard E. & Marshall, William L. (Eds.)

The Juvenile Sex Offender
Second Edition
New York: Guilford Press, 2008

BARRON, FRANK X., MONTUORI, ET AL. (EDS.)

CREATORS ON CREATING
Awakening and Cultivating the Imaginative Mind
(New Consciousness Reader)
New York: P. Tarcher/Putnam, 1997

BATESON, GREGORY

STEPS TO AN ECOLOGY OF MIND
Chicago: University of Chicago Press, 2000
Originally published in 1972

BENDER LAURETTA & BLAU, ABRAM

THE REACTION OF CHILDREN TO SEXUAL RELATIONS WITH ADULTS
American J. Orthopsychiatry 7 (1937), 500-518

BERNARD, FRITS

PAEDOPHILIA
A Factual Report
Amsterdam: Enclave, 1985

BERTALANFFY, LUDWIG VON

GENERAL SYSTEMS THEORY
Foundations, Development, Applications
New York: George Brazilier Publishing, 1976

BESANT, ANNIE

AN AUTOBIOGRAPHY
New Delhi: Penguin Books, 2005
Originally published in 1893

BETTELHEIM, BRUNO

A GOOD ENOUGH PARENT
New York: A. Knopf, 1987

THE USES OF ENCHANTMENT
New York: Vintage Books, 1989

BOHM, DAVID

WHOLENESS AND THE IMPLICATE ORDER
London: Routledge, 2002

THOUGHT AS A SYSTEM
London: Routledge, 1994

QUANTUM THEORY
London: Dover Publications, 1989

BOLDT, LAURENCE G.

ZEN AND THE ART OF MAKING A LIVING
A Practical Guide to Creative Career Design
New York: Penguin Arkana, 1993

HOW TO FIND THE WORK YOU LOVE
New York: Penguin Arkana, 1996

ZEN SOUP
Tasty Morsels of Zen Wisdom From Great Minds East & West
New York: Penguin Arkana, 1997

THE TAO OF ABUNDANCE
Eight Ancient Principles For Abundant Living
New York: Penguin Arkana, 1999

BORDEAUX-SZEKELY, EDMOND

TEACHING OF THE ESSENES FROM ENOCH TO THE DEAD
Sea Scrolls
Beekman Publishing, 1992

GOSPEL OF THE ESSENES
The Unknown Books of the Essenes
& Lost Scrolls of the Essene Brotherhood
Beekman Publishing, 1988

GOSPEL OF PEACE OF JESUS CHRIST
Beekman Publishing, 1994

GOSPEL OF PEACE, 2D VOL.
I B S International Publishers

BRANDEN, NATHANIEL

HOW TO RAISE YOUR SELF-ESTEEM
New York: Bantam, 1987

BRANT & TISZA

THE SEXUALLY MISUSED CHILD
American J. Orthopsychiatry, 47(1)(1977)

BULLOUGH & BULLOUGH (EDS.)

HUMAN SEXUALITY
An Encyclopedia
New York: Garland Publishing, 1994

SIN, SICKNESS AND SANITY
A History of Sexual Attitudes
New York: New American Library, 1977

BUXTON, RICHARD

THE COMPLETE WORLD OF GREEK MYTHOLOGY
London: Thames & Hudson, 2007

CAIN, CHELSEA & MOON UNIT ZAPPA

WILD CHILD
New York: Seal Press (Feminist Publishing), 1999

CALDERONE & RAMEY

TALKING WITH YOUR CHILD ABOUT SEX
New York: Random House, 1982

CAMPBELL, HERBERT JAMES

THE PLEASURE AREAS
London: Eyre Methuen Ltd., 1973

CAMPBELL, JACQUELINE C.

ASSESSING DANGEROUSNESS
Violence by Sexual Offenders, Batterers and Child
Abusers
New York: Sage Publications, 2004

CAMPBELL, JOSEPH

THE HERO WITH A THOUSAND FACES
Princeton: Princeton University Press, 1973
(Bollingen Series XVII)
London: Orion Books, 1999

OCCIDENTAL MYTHOLOGY
Princeton: Princeton University Press, 1973
(Bollingen Series XVII)
New York: Penguin Arkana, 1991

THE MASKS OF GOD
Oriental Mythology
New York: Penguin Arkana, 1992
Originally published 1962

THE POWER OF MYTH
With Bill Moyers
ed. by Sue Flowers
New York: Anchor Books, 1988

Capacchione, Lucia

The Power of Your Other Hand
North Hollywood, CA: Newcastle Publishing, 1988

Capra, Bernt Amadeus

Mindwalk
A Film for Passionate Thinkers
Based Upon Fritjof Capra's The Turning Point
New York: Triton Pictures, 1990

Capra, Fritjof

The Turning Point
Science, Society And The Rising Culture
New York: Simon & Schuster, 1987
Original Author Copyright, 1982

The Tao Of Physics
An Exploration of the Parallels Between Modern
Physics and Eastern Mysticism
New York: Shambhala Publications, 2000
(New Edition) Originally published in 1975

The Web Of Life
A New Scientific Understanding of Living Systems
New York: Doubleday, 1997
Author Copyright 1996

The Hidden Connections
New York: Doubleday, 2002

STEERING BUSINESS TOWARD SUSTAINABILITY
New York: United Nations University Press, 1995

UNCOMMON WISDOM
Conversations with Remarkable People
New York: Bantam, 1989

THE SCIENCE OF LEONARDO
Inside the Mind of the Great Genius of the Renaissance
New York: Anchor Books, 2008
New York: Bantam Doubleday, 2007 (First Publishing)

CASTANEDA, CARLOS

THE TEACHINGS OF DON JUAN
A Yaqui Way of Knowledge
Washington: Square Press, 1985

JOURNEY TO IXTLAN
Washington: Square Press: 1991

TALES OF POWER
Washington: Square Press, 1991

THE SECOND RING OF POWER
Washington: Square Press, 1991

CLARKE-STEWARD, S., FRIEDMAN, S. & KOCH, J.

CHILD DEVELOPMENT, A TOPICAL APPROACH
London: John Wiley, 1986

CONSTANTINE, LARRY L.

CHILDREN & SEX
New Findings, New Perspectives
Larry L. Constantine & Floyd M. Martinson (Eds.)
Boston: Little, Brown & Company, 1981

TREASURES OF THE ISLAND
Children in Alternative Lifestyles
Beverly Hills: Sage Publications, 1976

WHERE ARE THE KIDS?
in: Libby & Whitehurst (ed.)
Marriage and Alternatives
Glenview: Scott Foresman, 1977

OPEN FAMILY
A Lifestyle for Kids and other People
26 FAMILY COORDINATOR 113-130 (1977)

COOK, M. & HOWELLS, K. (EDS.)

ADULT SEXUAL INTEREST IN CHILDREN
Academic Press, London, 1980

COVITZ, JOEL

EMOTIONAL CHILD ABUSE
The Family Curse
Boston: Sigo Press, 1986

Currier, Richard L.

Juvenile Sexuality in Global Perspective
in : Children & Sex, New Findings, New Perspectives
Larry L. Constantine & Floyd M. Martinson (Eds.)
Boston: Little, Brown & Company, 1981

De Bono, Edward

The Use of Lateral Thinking
New York: Penguin, 1967

The Mechanism of Mind
New York: Penguin, 1969

Sur/Petition
London: HarperCollins, 1993

Tactics
London: HarperCollins, 1993
First published in 1985

Serious Creativity
Using the Power of Lateral Thinking to Create New Ideas
London: HarperCollins, 1996

Delacour, Jean-Baptiste

Glimpses of the Beyond
New York: Bantam Dell, 1975

DeMause, Lloyd

The History of Childhood
New York, 1974

Foundations of Psychohistory
New York: Creative Roots, 1982

Diamond, Stephen A., May, Rollo

Anger, Madness, and the Daimonic
The Psychological Genesis of Violence, Evil and Creativity
New York: State University of New York Press, 1999

DiCarlo, Russell E. (Ed.)

Towards A New World View
Conversations at the Leading Edge
Erie, PA: Epic Publishing, 1996

Dolto, Françoise

La Cause des Enfants
Paris: Laffont, 1985

Psychanalyse et Pédiatrie
Paris: Seuil, 1971

Séminaire de Psychanalyse d'Enfants, 1
Paris: Seuil, 1982

Séminaire de Psychanalyse d'Enfants, 2
Paris: Seuil, 1985

SÉMINAIRE DE PSYCHANALYSE D'ENFANTS, 3
Paris: Seuil, 1988

L'ÉVANGILE AU RISQUE DE LA PSYCHANALYSE
Paris: Seuil, 1980

DÜRCKHEIM, KARLFRIED GRAF

HARA: THE VITAL CENTER OF MAN
Rochester: Inner Traditions, 2004

ZEN AND US
New York: Penguin Arkana 1991

THE CALL FOR THE MASTER
New York: Penguin Books, 1993

ABSOLUTE LIVING
The Otherworldly in the World and the Path to Maturity
New York: Penguin Arkana, 1992

THE WAY OF TRANSFORMATION
Daily Life as a Spiritual Exercise
London: Allen & Unwin, 1988

THE JAPANESE CULT OF TRANQUILITY
London: Rider, 1960

EDMUNDS, FRANCIS

AN INTRODUCTION TO ANTHROPOSOPHY
Rudolf Steiner's Worldview
London: Rudolf Steiner Press, 2005

EDWARDES, A.

THE JEWEL OF THE LOTUS
New York, 1959

EINSTEIN, ALBERT

THE WORLD AS I SEE IT
New York: Citadel Press, 1993

OUT OF MY LATER YEARS
New York: Outlet, 1993

IDEAS AND OPINIONS
New York: Bonanza Books, 1988

ALBERT EINSTEIN NOTEBOOK
London: Dover Publications, 1989

EISLER, RIANE

THE CHALICE AND THE BLADE
Our history, Our future
San Francisco: Harper & Row, 1995

SACRED PLEASURE: SEX, MYTH AND THE POLITICS OF THE BODY
New Paths to Power and Love
San Francisco: Harper & Row, 1996

THE PARTNERSHIP WAY
New Tools for Living and Learning
With David Loye
Brandon, VT: Holistic Education Press, 1998

ELWIN, V.

THE MURIA AND THEIR GHOTUL
Bombay: Oxford University Press, 1947

THE SECRET LIFE OF WATER
New York: Atria Books, 2005

ERICKSON, MILTON H.

MY VOICE WILL GO WITH YOU
The Teaching Tales of Milton H. Erickson
by Sidney Rosen (Ed.)
New York: Norton & Co., 1991

COMPLETE WORKS 1.0, CD-ROM
New York: Milton H. Erickson Foundation, 2001

ERIKSON, ERIK H.

CHILDHOOD AND SOCIETY
New York: Norton, 1993
First published in 1950

EVANS-WENTZ, WALTER YEELING

THE FAIRY FAITH IN CELTIC COUNTRIES
London: Frowde, 1911
Republished by Dover Publications
(Minneola, New York), 2002

FARSON, RICHARD

BIRTHRIGHTS
A Bill of Rights for Children
Macmillan, New York, 1974

FEINBERG, JOEL

HARMLESS WRONGDOING
The Moral Limits of the Criminal Law, Vol. 4
New York: Oxford University Press, 1990

FENSTERHALM, HERBERT

DON'T SAY YES WHEN YOU WANT TO SAY NO
With Jean Bear
New York: Dell, 1980

FINKELHOR, DAVID

SEXUALLY VICTIMIZED CHILDREN
New York: Free Press, 1981

FINKELSTEIN, HAIM N. (ED.)

THE COLLECTED WRITINGS OF SALVADOR DALI
Cambridge: Cambridge University Press, 1998

FORTUNE, MARY M.

SEXUAL VIOLENCE
New York: Pilgrim Press, 1994

FOSTER/FREED

A BILL OF RIGHTS FOR CHILDREN
6 FAMILY LAW QUARTERLY 343 (1972)

FOUCAULT, MICHEL

THE HISTORY OF SEXUALITY, VOL. I : THE WILL TO KNOWLEDGE
London: Penguin, 1998
First published in 1976

THE HISTORY OF SEXUALITY, VOL. II : THE USE OF PLEASURE
London: Penguin, 1998
First published in 1984

THE HISTORY OF SEXUALITY, VOL. III : THE CARE OF SELF
London: Penguin, 1998
First published in 1984

FREUD, SIGMUND

THREE ESSAYS ON THE THEORY OF SEXUALITY
in: The Standard Edition of the Complete Psychological
Works of Sigmund Freud
London: Hogarth Press, 1953-54
Vol. 7, pp. 130 ff
(first published in 1905)

THE INTERPRETATION OF DREAMS
New York: Avon, Reissue Edition, 1980
and in: The Standard Edition of the Complete Psychological
Works of Sigmund Freud , (24 Volumes) ed. by James Strachey
New York: W. W. Norton & Company, 1976

TOTEM AND TABOO
New York: Routledge, 1999
Originally published in 1913

FREUND, KURT

ASSESSMENT OF PEDOPHILIA
in: Cook, M. and Howells, K. (eds.)
Adult Sexual Interest in Children
Academic Press, London, 1980

FROMM, ERICH

THE ANATOMY OF HUMAN DESTRUCTIVENESS
New York: Owl Book, 1992
Originally published in 1973

ESCAPE FROM FREEDOM
New York: Owl Books, 1994
Originally published in 1941

TO HAVE OR TO BE
New York: Continuum International Publishing, 1996
Originally published in 1976

THE ART OF LOVING
New York: HarperPerennial, 2000
Originally published in 1956

GELDARD, RICHARD

REMEMBERING HERACLITUS
New York: Lindisfarne Books, 2000

GERBER, RICHARD

A PRACTICAL GUIDE TO VIBRATIONAL MEDICINE
Energy Healing and Spiritual Transformation
New York: Harper & Collins, 2001

GELLER, URI

THE MINDPOWER KIT
Includes Book, Audiotape, Quartz Crystal And Meditation Circle
New York: Penguin, 1996

GESELL, IZZY

PLAYING ALONG
37 Group Learning Activities Borrowed from Improvisational Theater
Whole Person Associates, 1997

GHISELIN, BREWSTER (ED.)

THE CREATIVE PROCESS
Reflections on Invention in the Arts and Sciences
Berkeley: University of California Press, 1985
First published in 1952

GIBSON, IAN

THE SHAMEFUL LIFE OF SALVADOR DALI
New York: Norton, 1998

GIL, DAVID G.

SOCIETAL VIOLENCE AND VIOLENCE IN FAMILIES
in: David G. Gil, Child Abuse and Violence
New York: Ams Press, 1928

GIMBUTAS, MARIJA

THE LANGUAGE OF THE GODDESS
London: Thames & Hudson, 2001

GOLDENSTEIN, JOYCE

EINSTEIN: PHYSICIST AND GENIUS
(Great Minds of Science)
New York: Enslow Publishers, 1995

GOLDMAN, JONATHAN & GOLDMAN, ANDI

TANTRA OF SOUND
Frequencies of Healing
Charlottesville: Hampton Roads, 2005

HEALING SOUNDS
The Power of Harmonies
Rochester: Healing Arts Press, 2002

HEALING SOUNDS
Principles of Sound Healing
DVD, 90 min.
Sacred Mysteries, 2004

GOLDSTEIN, JEFFREY H.

AGGRESSION AND CRIMES OF VIOLENCE
New York, 1975

GOLEMAN, DANIEL

EMOTIONAL INTELLIGENCE
New York, Bantam Books, 1995

GORDON, ROSEMARY

PEDOPHILIA: NORMAL AND ABNORMAL
in: Kraemer, The Forbidden Love
London, 1976

GORDON WASSON, R.

THE ROAD TO ELEUSIS
Unveiling the Secret of the Mysteries
With Albert Hofmann, Huston Smith, Carl Ruck and Peter
Webster
Berkeley, CA: North Atlantic Books, 2008

BIBLIOGRAPHY

GOSWAMI, AMIT

THE SELF-AWARE UNIVERSE
How Consciousness Creates the Material World
New York: Tarcher/Putnam, 1995

GOTTLIEB, ADAM

PEYOTE AND OTHER PSYCHOACTIVE CACTI
Ronin Publishing, 2nd edition, 1997

GROF, STANISLAV

ANCIENT WISDOM AND MODERN SCIENCE
New York: State University of New York Press, 1984

BEYOND THE BRAIN
Birth, Death and Transcendence in Psychotherapy
New York: State University of New York, 1985

LSD: DOORWAY TO THE NUMINOUS
The Groundbreaking Psychedelic Research into Realms of the
Human Unconscious
Rochester: Park Street Press, 2009

REALMS OF THE HUMAN UNCONSCIOUS
Observations from LSD Research
New York: E.P. Dutton, 1976

THE COSMIC GAME
Explorations of the Frontiers of Human Consciousness
New York: State University of New York Press, 1998

THE HOLOTROPIC MIND
The Three Levels of Human Consciousness
With Hal Zina Bennett
New York: HarperCollins, 1993

WHEN THE IMPOSSIBLE HAPPENS
Adventures in Non-Ordinary Reality
Louisville, CO: Sounds True, 2005

HOUSTON, JEAN

THE POSSIBLE HUMAN
A Course in Enhancing Your Physical, Mental, and Creative Abilities
New York: Jeremy P. Tarcher/Putnam, 1982

HOWELLS, KEVIN

ADULT SEXUAL INTEREST IN CHILDREN
Considerations Relevant to Theories of Aetiology in:
Cook, M. and Howells, K. (eds.): Adult Sexual Interest in Children
Academic Press, London, 1980

HUNT, VALERIE

INFINITE MIND
Science of the Human Vibrations of Consciousness
Malibu, CA: Malibu Publishing, 2000

INNOCENTI DECLARATION

DECLARATION ON THE PROTECTION, PROMOTION AND SUPPORT OF BREASTFEEDING
http://www.innocenti15.net/inno.htm

JACKSON, NIGEL

THE RUNE MYSTERIES
With Silver RavenWolf
St. Paul, Minn.: Llewellyn Publications, 2000

JACKSON, STEVI

CHILDHOOD AND SEXUALITY
New York: Blackwell, 1982

JAFFE, HANS L.C.

PICASSO
New York: Abradale Press, 1996

JAMES, WILLIAM

WRITINGS 1902-1910
The Varieties of Religious Experience / Pragmatism / A Pluralistic
Universe / The Meaning of Truth / Some Problems of Philosophy
/ Essays
New York: Library of America, 1988

JANOV, ARTHUR

PRIMAL MAN
The New Consciousness
New York: Crowell, 1975

JOHNSON, PAUL

A HISTORY OF THE JEWS
New York: Harper & Row, 1987

JOHNSTON & DEISHER

CONTEMPORARY COMMUNAL CHILD REARING: A FIRST ANALYSIS
52 PEDIATRICS 319 (1973)

JONES, W.H.S., LITT, D.

PLINY NATURAL HISTORY
Cambridge, Mass.: Harvard University Press, 1980

JUNG, CARL GUSTAV

ARCHETYPES OF THE COLLECTIVE UNCONSCIOUS
in: The Basic Writings of C.G. Jung
New York: The Modern Library, 1959, 358-407

COLLECTED WORKS
New York, 1959

ON THE NATURE OF THE PSYCHE
in: The Basic Writings of C.G. Jung

New York: The Modern Library, 1959, 47-133

PSYCHOLOGICAL TYPES
Collected Writings, Vol. 6
Princeton: Princeton University Press, 1971

PSYCHOLOGY AND RELIGION
in: The Basic Writings of C.G. Jung
New York: The Modern Library, 1959, 582-655

RELIGIOUS AND PSYCHOLOGICAL PROBLEMS OF ALCHEMY
in: The Basic Writings of C.G. Jung
New York: The Modern Library, 1959, 537-581

SYMBOL UND LIBIDO
Freiburg: Walter Verlag, 1987

THE BASIC WRITINGS OF C.G. JUNG
New York: The Modern Library, 1959

THE DEVELOPMENT OF PERSONALITY
Collected Writings, Vol. 17
Princeton: Princeton University Press, 1954

THE MEANING AND SIGNIFICANCE OF DREAMS
Boston: Sigo Press, 1991

THE MYTH OF THE DIVINE CHILD
in: Essays on A Science of Mythology
Princeton, N.J.: Princeton University Press Bollingen
Series XXII, 1969. (With Karl Kerenyi)

TWO ESSAYS ON ANALYTICAL PSYCHOLOGY
Collected Writings, Vol. 7
Princeton: Princeton University Press, 1972
First published by Routledge & Kegan Paul, Ltd., 1953

KAHN, CHARLES (ED.)

THE ART AND THOUGHT OF HERACLITUS
Cambridge: Cambridge University Press, 2008

KAPLEAU, ROSHI PHILIP

THREE PILLARS OF ZEN
Boston: Beacon Press, 1967

KARAGULLA, SHAFICA

THE CHAKRAS
Correlations between Medical Science and Clairvoyant
Observation (With Dora van Gelder Kunz)
Wheaton: Quest Books, 1989

KLEIN, MELANIE

LOVE, GUILT AND REPARATION, AND OTHER WORKS 1921-1945
New York: Free Press, 1984
(Reissue Edition)

ENVY AND GRATITUDE AND OTHER WORKS 1946-1963
New York: Free Press, 2002
(Reissue Edition)

KRAEMER

THE FORBIDDEN LOVE
London, 1976

BIBLIOGRAPHY

KRAFFT-EBING, RICHARD VON

PSYCHOPATHIA SEXUALIS
New York: Bell Publishing, 1965
Originally published in 1886

KRAUSE, DONALD G.

THE ART OF WAR FOR EXECUTIVES
London: Nicholas Brealey Publishing, 1995

KRISHNAMURTI, J.

FREEDOM FROM THE KNOWN
San Francisco: Harper & Row, 1969

THE FIRST AND LAST FREEDOM
San Francisco: Harper & Row, 1975

EDUCATION AND THE SIGNIFICANCE OF LIFE
London: Victor Gollancz, 1978

COMMENTARIES ON LIVING
First Series
London: Victor Gollancz, 1985

COMMENTARIES ON LIVING
Second Series
London: Victor Gollancz, 1986

KRISHNAMURTI'S JOURNAL
London: Victor Gollancz, 1987

KRISHNAMURTI'S NOTEBOOK
London: Victor Gollancz, 1986

BEYOND VIOLENCE
London: Victor Gollancz, 1985

BEGINNINGS OF LEARNING
New York: Penguin, 1986

THE PENGUIN KRISHNAMURTI READER
New York: Penguin, 1987

ON GOD
San Francisco: Harper & Row, 1992

ON FEAR
San Francisco: Harper & Row, 1995

THE ESSENTIAL KRISHNAMURTI
San Francisco: Harper & Row, 1996

THE ENDING OF TIME
With Dr. David Bohm
San Francisco: Harper & Row, 1985

LAING, RONALD DAVID

DIVIDED SELF
New York: Viking Press, 1991

R.D. LAING AND THE PATHS OF ANTI-PSYCHIATRY
ed., by Z. Kotowicz
London: Routledge, 1997

THE POLITICS OF EXPERIENCE
New York: Pantheon, 1983

BIBLIOGRAPHY

LAKHOVSKY, GEORGES

SECRET OF LIFE
New York: Kessinger Publishing, 2003

LASZLO, ERVIN

SCIENCE AND THE AKASHIC FIELD
An Integral Theory of Everything
Rochester: Inner Traditions, 2004

QUANTUM SHIFT TO THE GLOBAL BRAIN
How the New Scientific Reality Can Change Us and Our World
Rochester: Inner Traditions, 2008

SCIENCE AND THE REENCHANTMENT OF THE COSMOS
The Rise of the Integral Vision of Reality
Rochester: Inner Traditions, 2006

THE AKASHIC EXPERIENCE
Science and the Cosmic Memory Field
Rochester: Inner Traditions, 2009

THE CHAOS POINT
The World at the Crossroads
Newburyport, MA: Hampton Roads Publishing, 2006

LAUD, ANNE & GILSTROP, MAY

VIOLENCE IN THE FAMILY
A Selected Bibliography on Child Abuse, Sexual Abuse of
Children & Domestic Violence, June 1985, University of Georgia
Libraries, Bibliographical Series, No. 32

LEADBEATER, CHARLES WEBSTER

ASTRAL PLANE
Its Scenery, Inhabitants and Phenomena
Kessinger Publishing Reprint Edition, 1997

DREAMS
What they Are and How they are Caused
London: Theosophical Publishing Society, 1903
Kessinger Publishing Reprint Edition, 1998

THE INNER LIFE
Chicago: The Rajput Press, 1911
Kessinger Publishing

LEARY, TIMOTHY

OUR BRAIN IS GOD
Berkeley, CA: Ronin Publishing, 2001
Author Copyright 1988

LEBOYER, FREDERICK

BIRTH WITHOUT VIOLENCE
New York, 1975

INNER BEAUTY, INNER LIGHT
New York: Newmarket Press, 1997

LOVING HANDS
The Traditional Art of Baby Massage
New York: Newmarket Press, 1977

The Art of Breathing
New York: Newmarket Press, 1991

Leggett, Trevor P.

A First Zen Reader
Rutland: C.E. Tuttle, 1980
Originally published in 1972

Leonard, George, Murphy, Michael

The Live We Are Given
A Long Term Program for Realizing the
Potential of Body, Mind, Heart and Soul
New York: Jeremy P. Tarcher/Putnam, 1984

Licht, Hans

Sexual Life in Ancient Greece
New York: AMS Press, 1995

Liedloff, Jean

Continuum Concept
In Search of Happiness Lost
New York: Perseus Books, 1986
First published in 1977

LIPTON, BRUCE

THE BIOLOGY OF BELIEF
Unleashing the Power of Consciousness, Matter and Miracles
Santa Rosa, CA: Mountain of Love/Elite Books, 2005

LOCKE, JOHN

SOME THOUGHTS CONCERNING EDUCATION
London, 1690
Reprinted in: The Works of John Locke, 1823
Vol. IX., pp. 6-205

LONG, MAX FREEDOM

THE SECRET SCIENCE AT WORK
The Huna Method as a Way of Life
Marina del Rey: De Vorss Publications, 1995
Originally published in 1953

GROWING INTO LIGHT
A Personal Guide to Practicing the Huna Method,
Marina del Rey: De Vorss Publications, 1955

LOWEN, ALEXANDER

BIOENERGETICS
New York: Coward, McGoegham 1975

DEPRESSION AND THE BODY
The Biological Basis of Faith and Reality
New York: Penguin, 1992

FEAR OF LIFE
New York: Bioenergetic Press, 2003

HONORING THE BODY
The Autobiography of Alexander Lowen
New York: Bioenergetic Press, 2004

JOY
The Surrender to the Body and to Life
New York: Penguin, 1995

LOVE AND ORGASM
New York: Macmillan, 1965

LOVE, SEX AND YOUR HEART
New York: Bioenergetics Press, 2004

NARCISSISM: DENIAL OF THE TRUE SELF
New York: Macmillan, Collier Books, 1983

PLEASURE: A CREATIVE APPROACH TO LIFE
New York: Bioenergetics Press, 2004
First published in 1970

THE LANGUAGE OF THE BODY
Physical Dynamics of Character Structure
New York: Bioenergetics Press, 2006

MALINOWSKI, BRONISLAW

CRIME UND CUSTOM IN SAVAGE SOCIETY
London: Kegan, 1926

SEX AND REPRESSION IN SAVAGE SOCIETY
London: Kegan, 1927

THE SEXUAL LIFE OF SAVAGES IN NORTH WEST MELANESIA
New York: Halycon House, 1929

MANN, EDWARD W.

ORGONE, REICH & EROS
Wilhelm Reich's Theory of Life Energy
New York: Simon & Schuster (Touchstone), 1973

MARTINSON, FLOYD M.

SEXUAL KNOWLEDGE
Values and Behavior Patterns
St. Peter: Minn.: Gustavus Adolphus College, 1966

INFANT AND CHILD SEXUALITY
St. Peter: Minn.: Gustavus Adolphus College, 1973

THE QUALITY OF ADOLESCENT EXPERIENCES
St. Peter: Minn.: Gustavus Adolphus College, 1974

THE CHILD AND THE FAMILY
Calgary, Alberta: The University of Calgary, 1980

THE SEX EDUCATION OF YOUNG CHILDREN
in: Lorna Brown (Ed.), Sex Education in the Eighties
New York, London: Plenum Press, 1981, pp. 51 ff.

THE SEXUAL LIFE OF CHILDREN
New York: Bergin & Garvey, 1994

CHILDREN AND SEX, PART II: CHILDHOOD SEXUALITY
in: Bullough & Bullough, Human Sexuality (1994)
Pp. 111-116

MASTERS, R.E.L.

FORBIDDEN SEXUAL BEHAVIOR AND MORALITY
New York, 1962

MCCAREY, WILLIAM A.

IN SEARCH OF HEALING
Whole-Body Healing Through the Mind-Body-Spirit Connection
New York: Berkley Publishing, 1996

MCLEOD, KEMBREW

FREEDOM OF EXPRESSION
Resistance and Repression in the Age of Intellectual Property
Minneapolis, MN: University of Minnesota Press, 2007

MCTAGGART, LYNNE

THE FIELD
The Quest for the Secret Force of the Universe
New York: Harper & Collins, 2002

MEAD, MARGARET

SEX AND TEMPERAMENT IN THREE PRIMITIVE SOCIETIES
New York, 1935

MEADOWS, DONELLA H.

THINKING IN SYSTEMS
A Primer
White River, VT: Chelsea Green Publishing, 2008

MEHTA, ROHIT

J. KRISHNAMURTI AND THE NAMELESS EXPERIENCE
A Comprehensive Discussion of J. Krishnamurti's Approach to Life
Delhi: Motilal Banarsidass Publishers, 2002

MERLEAU-PONTY, MAURICE

PHENOMENOLOGY OF PERCEPTION
London: Routledge, 1995
Originally published 1945

METZNER, RALPH (ED.)

AYAHUASCA, HUMAN CONSCIOUSNESS AND THE SPIRITS OF NATURE
ed. by Ralph Metzner, Ph.D
New York: Thunder's Mouth Press, 1999

THE PSYCHEDELIC EXPERIENCE
A Manual Based on the Tibetan Book of the Dead
With Timothy Leary and Richard Alpert
New York: Citadel, 1995

Miller, Alice

Four Your Own Good
Hidden Cruelty in Child-Rearing and the Roots of Violence
New York: Farrar, Straus & Giroux, 1983

Pictures of a Childhood
New York: Farrar, Straus & Giroux, 1986

The Drama of the Gifted Child
In Search for the True Self
translated by Ruth Ward
New York: Basic Books, 1996

Thou Shalt Not Be Aware
Society's Betrayal of the Child
New York: Noonday, 1998

The Political Consequences of Child Abuse
in: The Journal of Psychohistory 26, 2 (Fall 1998)

Moll, Albert

The Sexual Life of the Child
New York: Macmillan, 1912
First published in German as
Das Sexualleben des Kindes, 1909

Monroe, Robert

Ultimate Journey
New York: Broadway Books, 1994

MONTAGU, ASHLEY

TOUCHING
The Human Significance of the Skin
New York: Harper & Row, 1978

MONTESSORI, MARIA

THE ABSORBENT MIND
Reprint Edition
New York: Buccaneer Books, 1995
First published in 1973

MOORE, THOMAS

CARE OF THE SOUL
A Guide for Cultivating Depth and Sacredness in Everyday Life
New York: Harper & Collins, 1994

MOSER, CHARLES ALLEN

DSM-IV-TR AND THE PARAPHILIAS: AN ARGUMENT FOR REMOVAL
With Peggy J. Kleinplatz
Journal of Psychology and Human Sexuality 17 (3/4), 91-109
(2005)

MURDOCK, G.

SOCIAL STRUCTURE
New York: Macmillan, 1960

MURPHY, JOSEPH

THE POWER OF YOUR SUBCONSCIOUS MIND
West Nyack, N.Y.: Parker, 1981, N.Y.: Bantam, 1982
Originally published in 1962

THE MIRACLE OF MIND DYNAMICS
New York: Prentice Hall, 1964

MIRACLE POWER FOR INFINITE RICHES
West Nyack, N.Y.: Parker, 1972

THE AMAZING LAWS OF COSMIC MIND POWER
West Nyack, N.Y.: Parker, 1973

SECRETS OF THE I CHING
West Nyack, N.Y.: Parker, 1970

THINK YOURSELF RICH
Use the Power of Your Subconscious Mind to Find True Wealth
Revised by Ian D. McMahan, Ph.D.
Paramus, NJ: Reward Books, 2001

MURPHY, MICHAEL

THE FUTURE OF THE BODY
Explorations into the Further Evolution of Human Nature
New York: Jeremy P. Tarcher/Putnam, 1992

MYERS, TONY PEARCE

THE SOUL OF CREATIVITY
Insights into the Creative Process
Novato, CA: New World Library, 1999

MYSS, CAROLINE

THE CREATION OF HEALTH
The Emotional, Psychological, and Spiritual Responses that
Promote Health and Healing
New York: Three Rivers Press, 1998

NAPARSTEK, BELLERUTH

YOUR SIXTH SENSE
Unlocking the Power of Your Intuition
London: HarperCollins, 1998

STAYING WELL WITH GUIDED IMAGERY
New York: Warner Books, 1995

NARBY, JEREMY

THE COSMIC SERPENT
DNA and the Origins of Knowledge
New York: J. P. Tarcher, 1999

NAU, ERIKA

SELF-AWARENESS THROUGH HUNA
Virginia Beach: Donning, 1981

NEILL, ALEXANDER SUTHERLAND

NEILL! NEILL! ORANGE-PEEL!
New York: Hart Publishing Co., 1972

SUMMERHILL
A Radical Approach to Child Rearing
New York: Hart Publishing, Reprint 1984
Originally published 1960

SUMMERHILL SCHOOL
A New View of Childhood
New York: St. Martin's Press
Reprint 1995

NEUMANN, ERICH

THE GREAT MOTHER
Princeton: Princeton University Press, 1955
(Bollingen Series)

NEWTON, MICHAEL

LIFE BETWEEN LIVES
Hypnotherapy for Spiritual Regression
Woodbury, Minn.: Llewellyn Publications, 2006

NICHOLS, SALLIE

JUNG AND TAROT: AN ARCHETYPAL JOURNEY
New York: Red Wheel/Weiser, 1986

NIN, ANAÏS

THE DIARY OF ANAÏS NIN (7 VOLUMES)
New York, 1966

VOLUME 1 (1931-1934)
New York: Harvest Books, 1969

VOLUME 2 (1934-1939)
New York: Harvest Books, 1970

ODENT, MICHEL

BIRTH REBORN
What Childbirth Should Be
London: Souvenir Press, 1994

THE SCIENTIFICATION OF LOVE
London: Free Association Books, 1999

PRIMAL HEALTH
Understanding the Critical Period Between Conception
and the First Birthday
London: Clairview Books, 2002
First Published in 1986 with Century Hutchinson in London

THE FUNCTIONS OF THE ORGASMS
The Highway to Transcendence
London: Pinter & Martin, 2009

OLLENDORF-REICH, ILSE

WILHELM REICH, A PERSONAL BIOGRAPHY
New York, St. Martins Press, 1969

WILHELM REICH
Vorwort von A.S. Neill
München, Kindler, 1975

PEARCE MYERS, TONY (EDITOR)

THE SOUL OF CREATIVITY
Insights into the Creative Process
Novato: New World Library, 1999

PERT, CANDACE B.

MOLECULES OF EMOTION
The Science Behind Mind-Body Medicine
New York: Scribner, 2003

PETRASH, JACK

UNDERSTANDING WALDORF EDUCATION
Teaching from the Inside Out
London: Floris Books, 2003

PLUMMER, KENNETH

PEDOPHILIA
Constructing a Sociological Baseline
in: in: Cook, M. and Howells, K. (Eds.):
Adult Sexual Interest in Children
Academic Press, London, 1980, pp. 220 ff.

PORTEOUS, HEDY S.

SEX AND IDENTITY
Your Child's Sexuality
Indianapolis: Bobbs-Merrill, 1972

PRESCOTT, JAMES W.

AFFECTIONAL BONDING FOR THE PREVENTION OF VIOLENT BEHAVIORS
Neurobiological, Psychological and Religious/Spiritual
Determinants, in: Hertzberg, L.J., Ostrum, G.F. and Field, J.R.,
(Eds.)

VIOLENT BEHAVIOR
Vol. 1, Assessment & Intervention, Chapter Six
New York: PMA Publishing, 1990

ALIENATION OF AFFECTION
Psychology Today, December 1979

BODY PLEASURE AND THE ORIGINS OF VIOLENCE
Bulletin of the Atomic Scientists, 10-20 (1975)

DEPRIVATION OF PHYSICAL AFFECTION AS A PRIMARY PROCESS IN THE
DEVELOPMENT OF PHYSICAL VIOLENCE A COMPARATIVE AND
CROSS-CULTURAL PERSPECTIVE, IN: DAVID G. GIL, ED., CHILD ABUSE
AND VIOLENCE
New York: Ams Press, 1979

EARLY SOMATOSENSORY DEPRIVATION AS AN ONTOGENETIC PROCESS IN
THE ABNORMAL DEVELOPMENT OF THE BRAIN AND BEHAVIOR,
in: Medical Primatology, ed. by I.E. Goldsmith and J.
Moor-Jankowski,
New York: S. Karger, 1971

GENITAL MUTILATION OF CHILDREN: FAILURE OF HUMANITY AND
HUMANISM
Unprinted Essay (2005)
http://www.violence.de/prescott/letters/
CIRC_CONGRESS_MONTAGUE_9.30.05.html

GENITAL PAIN VS. GENITAL PLEASURE
Why the One and not the Other

BIBLIOGRAPHY

The Truth Seeker, July/August 1989, pp. 14-21
http://www.violence.de/prescott/truthseeker/genpl.html

HOW CULTURE SHAPES THE DEVELOPING BRAIN AND THE FUTURE OF
HUMANITY
A Brief Summary of the research which links brain abnormalities
and violence to an absence of nurturing and bonding very early
in childhood, in: Touch the Future: Optimum Learning
Relationships

FOR CHILDREN & ADULTS
Spring 2002 (Ed. by Michael Mendizza)
Nevada City, CA, 2002

INVITED COMMENTARY: CENTRAL NERVOUS SYSTEM FUNCTIONING IN
ALTERED SENSORY ENVIRONMENTS
in: M.H. Appley and R. Trumbull (Eds.), Psychological Stress,
New York: Appleton-Century Crofts, 1967

OUR TWO CULTURAL BRAINS: NEUROINTEGRATIVE AND
NEURODISSOCIATIVE
http://www.violence.de/prescott/letters/Our_Two_Cultural_Brain
s.pdf

PHYLOGENETIC AND ONTOGENETIC ASPECTS OF HUMAN AFFECTIONAL
DEVELOPMENT,
in: Progress in Sexology, Proceedings of the 1976 International,
Congress of Sexology, ed. by R. Gemme & C.C. Wheeler, New
York: Plenum Press, 1977

PREVENTION OR THERAPY AND THE POLITICS OF TRUST INSPIRING A NEW
HUMAN AGENDA
in: Psychotherapy and Politics International
Volume 3(3), pp. 194-211
London: John Wiley, 2005

SEX AND THE BRAIN
Midcontinent & Eastern Regions, June 13-16, 2002

Big Rapids, MI: Society for Cross-Cultural Research,
32nd Annual Meeting, 2005
http://www.violence.de/archive.shtml

SIXTEEN PRINCIPLES FOR PERSONAL, FAMILY AND GLOBAL PEACE
The Truth Seeker, March/April 1989
http://www.violence.de/prescott/letters/Sixteen_Principles.pdf

SOMATOSENSORY AFFECTIONAL DEPRIVATION (SAD) THEORY OF DRUG
AND ALCOHOL USE
in: Theories on Drug Abuse: Selected Contemporary
Perspectives, ed. by Dan J. Lettieri, Mollie Sayers and Helen
Wallenstien Pearson, NIDA Research Monograph 30, March
1980, Rockville, MD: National Institute on Drug Abuse,
Department of Health and Human Services, 1980

THE ORIGINS OF HUMAN LOVE AND VIOLENCE
Pre- and Perinatal Psychology Journal, Volume 10, Number 3:
Spring 1996, pp. 143-188The Origins of Love and Violence

SENSORY DEPRIVATION AND THE DEVELOPING BRAIN
Research and Prevention (DVD)
http://ttfuture.org/store/origins_orders
http://violence.de
http://ttfuture.org/violence
http://montagunocircpetition.org

PRITCHARD, COLIN

THE CHILD ABUSERS
New York: Open University Press, 2004

RAKNES, OLA

WILHELM REICH AND ORGONOMY
Oslo: Universitetsforlaget, 1970

RANDALL, NEVILLE

LIFE AFTER DEATH
London: Robert Hale, 1999

RANK, OTTO

ART AND ARTIST
With Charles Francis Atkinson and Anaïs Nin
New York: W.W. Norton, 1989
Originally published in 1932

THE SIGNIFICANCE OF PSYCHOANALYSIS FOR THE MENTAL SCIENCES
New York: BiblioBazaar, 2009
First published in 1913

REDFIELD, JAMES

THE TENTH INSIGHT
Holding the Vision
New York: Warner Books, 1996

THE CELESTINE PROPHECY
New York: Warner Books, 1995

REICH, WILHELM

A REVIEW OF THE THEORIES, DATING FROM THE 17TH CENTURY, ON THE ORIGIN OF ORGANIC LIFE
by Arthur Hahn, Literature Assistant at the Institut für Sexualökonomische Lebensforschung, Biologisches Laboratorium, Oslo, 1938, ©1979 Mary Boyd Higgins as Director of the Wilhelm Reich Infant Trust, XEROX Copy from the Wilhelm Reich Museum

CHILDREN OF THE FUTURE
On the Prevention of Sexual Pathology
New York: Farrar, Straus & Giroux, 1984
First published in 1950

CORE (COSMIC ORGONE ENGINEERING)
Part I, Space Ships, DOR and DROUGHT
©1984, Orgone Institute Press
XEROX Copy from the Wilhelm Reich Museum
Köln: Kiepenheuer & Witsch, 1987

EARLY WRITINGS 1
New York: Farrar, Straus & Giroux, 1975

ETHER, GOD & DEVIL & COSMIC SUPERIMPOSITION
New York: Farrar, Straus & Giroux, 1972
Originally published in 1949

GENITALITY IN THE THEORY AND THERAPY OF NEUROSIS
©1980 by Mary Boyd Higgins as Director of the Wilhelm Reich Infant Trust

PEOPLE IN TROUBLE
©1974 by Mary Boyd Higgins as Director of the Wilhelm Reich Infant Trust

BIBLIOGRAPHY

RECORD OF A FRIENDSHIP
The Correspondence of Wilhelm Reich and A. S. Neill
New York, Farrar, Straus & Giroux, 1981

SELECTED WRITINGS
An Introduction to Orgonomy
New York: Farrar, Straus & Giroux, 1973

THE BIOELECTRICAL INVESTIGATION OF SEXUALITY AND ANXIETY
New York: Farrar, Straus & Giroux, 1983
Originally published in 1935

THE BION EXPERIMENTS
reprinted in Selected Writings
New York: Farrar, Straus & Giroux, 1973

THE CANCER BIOPATHY (THE ORGONE, VOL. 2)
New York: Farrar, Straus & Giroux, 1973

THE FUNCTION OF THE ORGASM (THE ORGONE, VOL. 1)
Orgone Institute Press, New York, 1942

THE INVASION OF COMPULSORY SEX MORALITY
New York: Farrar, Straus & Giroux, 1971
Originally published in 1932

THE LEUKEMIA PROBLEM: APPROACH
©1951, Orgone Institute Press
Copyright Renewed 1979
XEROX Copy from the Wilhelm Reich Museum

THE MASS PSYCHOLOGY OF FASCISM
New York: Farrar, Straus & Giroux, 1970
Originally published in 1933

THE ORGONE ENERGY ACCUMULATOR
Its Scientific and Medical Use

©1951, 1979, Orgone Institute Press
XEROX Copy from the Wilhelm Reich Museum

THE SCHIZOPHRENIC SPLIT
©1945, 1949, 1972 by Mary Boyd Higgins as Director of the
Wilhelm Reich Infant Trust
XEROX Copy from the Wilhelm Reich Museum

THE SEXUAL REVOLUTION
©1945, 1962 by Mary Boyd Higgins as Director of the
Wilhelm Reich Infant Trust

RISO, DON RICHARD & HUDSON, RUSS

THE WISDOM OF THE ENNEAGRAM
The Complete Guide to Psychological and Spiritual Growth
For The Nine Personality Types
New York: Bantam Books, 1999

ROBBINS, ANTHONY

AWAKEN THE GIANT WITHIN
New York: Simon & Schuster, 1991

UNLIMITED POWER
The New Science of Personal Achievement
New York: Free Press, 1997

ROBERTS, JANE

THE NATURE OF PERSONAL REALITY
New York: Amber-Allen Publishing, 1994
First published in 1974

The Nature of the Psyche
Its Human Expression
New York, Amber-Allen Publishing, 1996
First published in 1979

Rosen, Sydney (Ed.)
____

My Voice Will Go With You
The Teaching Tales of Milton H. Erickson
New York: Norton & Co., 1991

Rothschild & Wolf
____

Children of the Counterculture
New York: Garden City, 1976

Sandfort, Theo
____

The Sexual Aspect of Pedophile Relations
The Experience of Twenty-five Boys
Amsterdam: Pan/Spartacus, 1982

Schlipp, Paul A. (Ed.)
____

Albert Einstein
Philosopher-Scientist
New York: Open Court Publishing, 1988

SCHWARTZ, ANDREW E.

GUIDED IMAGERY FOR GROUPS
Fifty Visualizations That Promote Relaxation, Problem-Solving,
Creativity, and Well-Being
Whole Person Associates, 1995

SHARAF, MYRON

FURY ON EARTH
A Biography of Wilhelm Reich
London: André Deutsch, 1983

SHELDRAKE, RUPERT

A NEW SCIENCE OF LIFE
The Hypothesis of Morphic Resonance
Rochester: Park Street Press, 1995

SHER, BARBARA & GOTTLIEB, ANNIE

WISHCRAFT
How to Get What You Really Want
2nd edition, New York: Ballantine Books, 2003

SHONE, RONALD

CREATIVE VISUALIZATION
Using Imagery and Imagination for Self-Transformation
New York: Destiny Books, 1998

SIMONTON, O. CARL ET AL.

GETTING WELL AGAIN
Los Angeles: Tarcher, 1978

SINGER, JUNE

ANDROGYNY
New York: Doubleday Dell, 1976

SMITH, C. MICHAEL

JUNG AND SHAMANISM IN DIALOGUE
London: Trafford Publishing, 2007

SPOCK, BENJAMIN

DR. SPOCK'S BABY AND CHILD CARE
8th Edition
New York: Pocket Books, 2004

STEIN, ROBERT M.

REDEEMING THE INNER CHILD IN MARRIAGE AND THERAPY
in: Reclaiming the Inner Child
ed. by Jeremiah Abrams
New York: Tarcher/Putnam, 1990, 261 ff.

STEINER, RUDOLF

THEOSOPHY
An Introduction to the Spiritual Processes in Human Life
and in the Cosmos
New York: Anthroposophic Press, 1994

STEKEL, WILHELM

AUTO-EROTICISM
A Psychiatric Study of Onanism and Neurosis
Republished, London: Paul Kegan, 2004

PATTERNS OF PSYCHOSEXUAL INFANTILISM
New York, 1959 (reprint edition)

SADISM AND MASOCHISM
New York: W.W. Norton & Co., 1953

SEX AND DREAMS
The Language of Dreams
Republished
New York: University Press of the Pacific, 2003

STIENE, BRONWEN & FRANS

THE REIKI SOURCEBOOK
New York: O Books, 2003

THE JAPANESE ART OF REIKI
A Practical Guide to Self-Healing
New York: O Books, 2005

STONE, HAL & STONE, SIDRA

EMBRACING OUR SELVES
The Voice Dialogue Manual
San Rafael, CA: New World Library, 1989

STRASSMAN, RICK

DMT: THE SPIRIT MOLECULE
A doctor's revolutionary research into the biology of near-death
and mystical experiences
Rochester: Park Street Press, 2001

SYMONDS, JOHN ADDINGTON

A PROBLEM IN GREEK ETHICS
New York: M.S.G. House, 1971

SZASZ, THOMAS

THE MYTH OF MENTAL ILLNESS
New York: Harper & Row, 1984

TALBOT, MICHAEL

THE HOLOGRAPHIC UNIVERSE
New York: HarperCollins, 1992

TARNAS, RICHARD

COSMOS AND PSYCHE
Intimations of a New World View
New York: Plume, 2007

THE PASSION OF THE WESTERN MIND
Understanding the Ideas that have Shaped Our World View
New York: Ballantine Books, 1993

TART, CHARLES T.

ALTERED STATES OF CONSCIOUSNESS
A Book of Readings
Hoboken, N.J.: Wiley & Sons, 1969

TEXTOR, R. B.

A CROSS-CULTURAL SUMMARY
New Haven, Human Relations Area Files (HRAF)
Press, 1967

THE ADVENT OF GREAT AWAKENING

A COURSE IN MIRACLES
Text Workbook and Manual for Teachers
New York: New Christian Church of Full Endeavor, 2007

TILLER, WILLIAM A.

CONSCIOUS ACTS OF CREATION
The Emergence of a New Physics
Associated Producers, 2004 (DVD)

PSYCHOENERGETIC SCIENCE
New York: Pavior, 2007

TOFFLER, ALVIN

POWERSHIFT
Knowledge, Wealth, and Violence at the Edge of the 21st
Century
New York: Bantam, 1991

REVOLUTIONARY WEALTH
How it will be created and how it will change our lives
New York: Broadway Business, 2007

THE THIRD WAVE
New York: Bantam, 1984

TOLLE, ECKHART

THE POWER OF NOW
A Guide to Spiritual Enlightenment
Novato, CA: New World Library, 2004

A NEW EARTH: AWAKENING TO YOUR LIFE'S PURPOSE
New York: Michael Joseph (Penguin), 2005

VAN GELDER, DORA

THE REAL WORLD OF FAIRIES
A First-Person Account
2nd Edition
Wheaton: Quest Books, 1999

VILLOLDO, ALBERTO

HEALING STATES
A Journey Into the World of Spiritual Healing and Shamanism
With Stanley Krippner
New York: Simon & Schuster (Fireside), 1987

DANCE OF THE FOUR WINDS: SECRETS OF THE INCA MEDICINE WHEEL
With Eric Jendresen
Rochester: Destiny Books, 1995

SHAMAN, HEALER, SAGE
How to Heal Yourself and Others with the Energy Medicine
of the Americas
New York: Harmony, 2000

HEALING THE LUMINOUS BODY
The Way of the Shaman with Dr. Alberto Villoldo
DVD, Sacred Mysteries Productions, 2004

MENDING THE PAST AND HEALING THE FUTURE WITH SOUL RETRIEVAL
New York: Hay House, 2005

WHITFIELD, CHARLES L.

HEALING THE CHILD WITHIN
Deerfield Beach, Fl: Health Communications, 1987

WHITING, BEATRICE B.

CHILDREN OF SIX CULTURES
A Psycho-Cultural Analysis
Cambridge: Harvard University Press, 1975

WILBER, KEN

SEX, ECOLOGY, SPIRITUALITY
The Spirit of Evolution
Boston: Shambhala, 2000

QUANTUM QUESTIONS
Mystical Writings of The World's Greatest Physicists
Boston: Shambhala, 2001

WILLIAMS, STREPHON KAPLAN

DREAMS AND SPIRITUAL GROWTH
With Patricia H. Berne and Louis M. Savary
New York: Paulist Press, 1984

DREAM CARDS
Understand Your Dreams and Enrich Your Life
New York: Simon & Schuster (Fireside), 1991

WOLF, FRED ALAN

TAKING THE QUANTUM LEAP
The New Physics for Nonscientists
New York: Harper & Row, 1989

PARALLEL UNIVERSES
New York: Simon & Schuster, 1990

THE DREAMING UNIVERSE
A Mind-Expanding Journey into the Realm Where Psyche and
Physics Meet
New York: Touchstone, 1995

THE EAGLE'S QUEST
A Physicist Finds the Scientific Truth At the Heart of the
Shamanic World
New York: Touchstone, 1997

YATES, ALAYNE

SEX WITHOUT SHAME: ENCOURAGING THE CHILD'S HEALTHY SEXUAL
DEVELOPMENT
New York, 1978
Republished Internet Edition

ZUKAV, GARY

THE DANCING WU LI MASTERS
An Overview of the New Physics
New York: HarperOne, 2001

PERSONAL NOTES